AF263695

LETTER TRACING AND HANDWRITING WORKBOOK FOR KIDS

Letters, Words, Sentence, Activities and More!

TABLE OF CONTENTS

INTRODUCTION

Welcome to the ***"Letter Tracing and Handwriting Workbook for Kids"*** – a comprehensive guide designed to enhance your child's foundational skills in writing and literacy. This workbook is thoughtfully crafted to engage young minds in a fun and educational journey, fostering essential skills that lay the groundwork for effective communication and language development.

In the early stages of a child's education, mastering the art of handwriting is a crucial milestone. This workbook is tailored to make this process enjoyable and interactive. Through a variety of engaging activities, your child will embark on a learning adventure that covers a range of fundamental skills.

Exploring the Contents:

- ***Tracing Skills:*** *The workbook begins with tracing exercises, providing a hands-on approach to improve fine motor skills and hand-eye coordination. These activities serve as a foundation for the more intricate writing tasks to come.*

- ***Trace and Write (Uppercase & Lowercase letters):*** *Dive into the fascinating world of letters. This section focuses on individual letters, both uppercase and lowercase, providing a comprehensive foundation for writing proficiency.*

- ***Trace the Words:*** *Transitioning from individual letters to complete words, this section encourages learners to trace and familiarize themselves with various words. The gradual progression ensures a seamless transition in building their vocabulary and writing skills.*

- ***Sentence Writing:*** *Elevate the experience by venturing into sentence construction. As children progress, they'll discover the joy of expressing thoughts coherently through written language.*

- ***Activity Pages (Coloring, Dot to Dots, Jumbled Words, Word Search):*** *Learning is not confined to tracing and writing alone. Our workbook introduces stimulating activities like coloring, dot-to-dots, jumbled words, and word searches, making the learning process enjoyable and holistic.*

Why Choose This Workbook:

- **Engaging Activities:** Every page is a new adventure, blending education with play to captivate young minds.

- **Progressive Learning:** The workbook is structured to provide a gradual progression from basic tracing to more complex writing exercises, ensuring a smooth learning curve.

- **Designed for Fun:** We believe that a child's first introduction to writing should be enjoyable. Our workbook infuses joy into the learning process, fostering a positive attitude towards language development.

As your child progresses through each section, celebrate their achievements, no matter how small. This workbook is not just a learning tool; it's a journey of growth, discovery, and accomplishment. Let the ***"Letter Tracing and Handwriting Workbook for Kids"*** be the stepping stone to a lifelong love of language and the written word.

Happy learning!

LET'S LEARN
Tracing Skills

Practice drawing lines by tracing on the dotted lines.

LET'S LEARN
Tracing Skills

Practice drawing lines by tracing on the dotted lines.

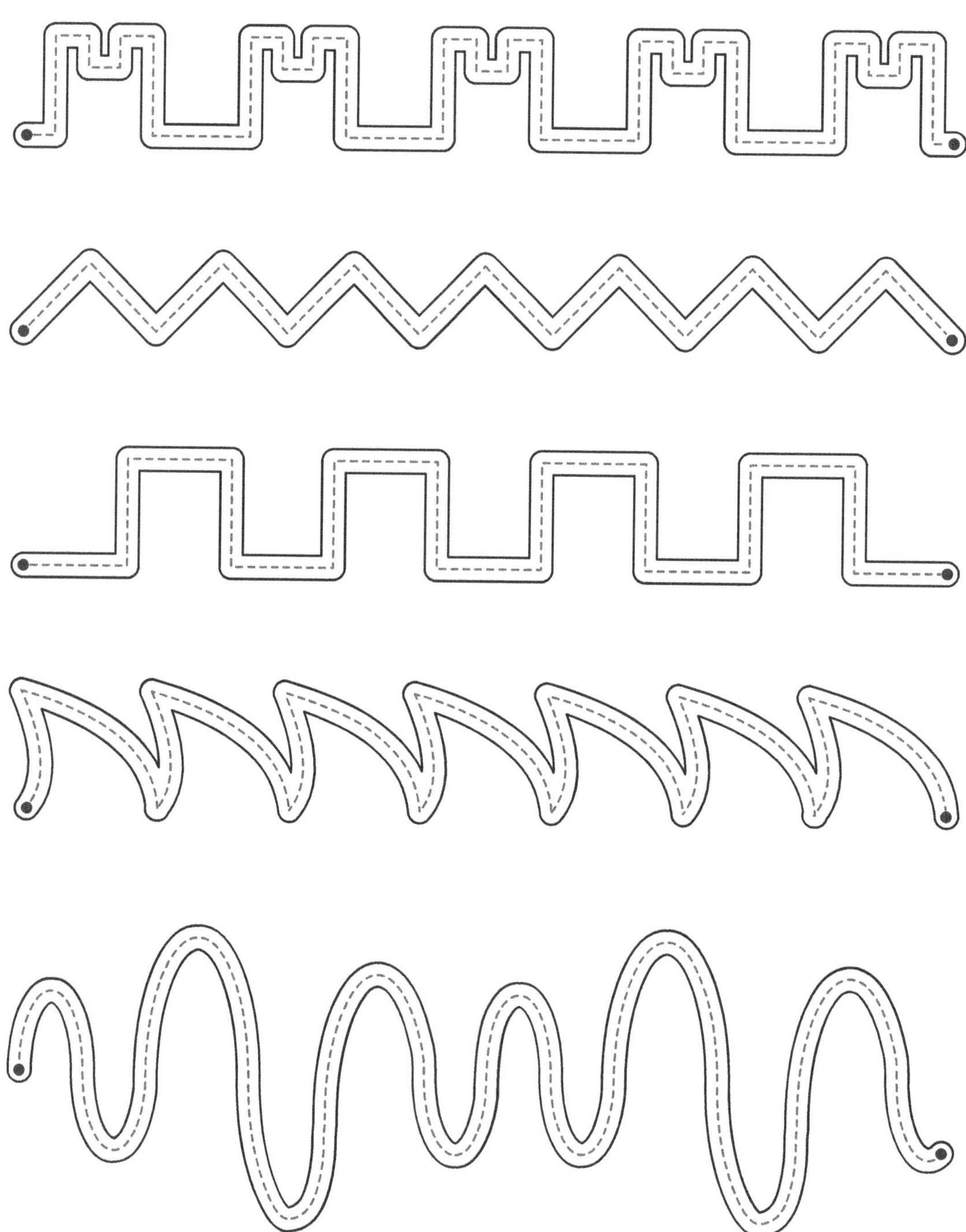

LET'S LEARN
Tracing Skills

Practice drawing lines by tracing on the dotted lines.

LET'S LEARN
Tracing Skills

Practice drawing lines by tracing on the dotted lines.

LET'S LEARN
Tracing Skills

Trace the line from the monkey to the banana.

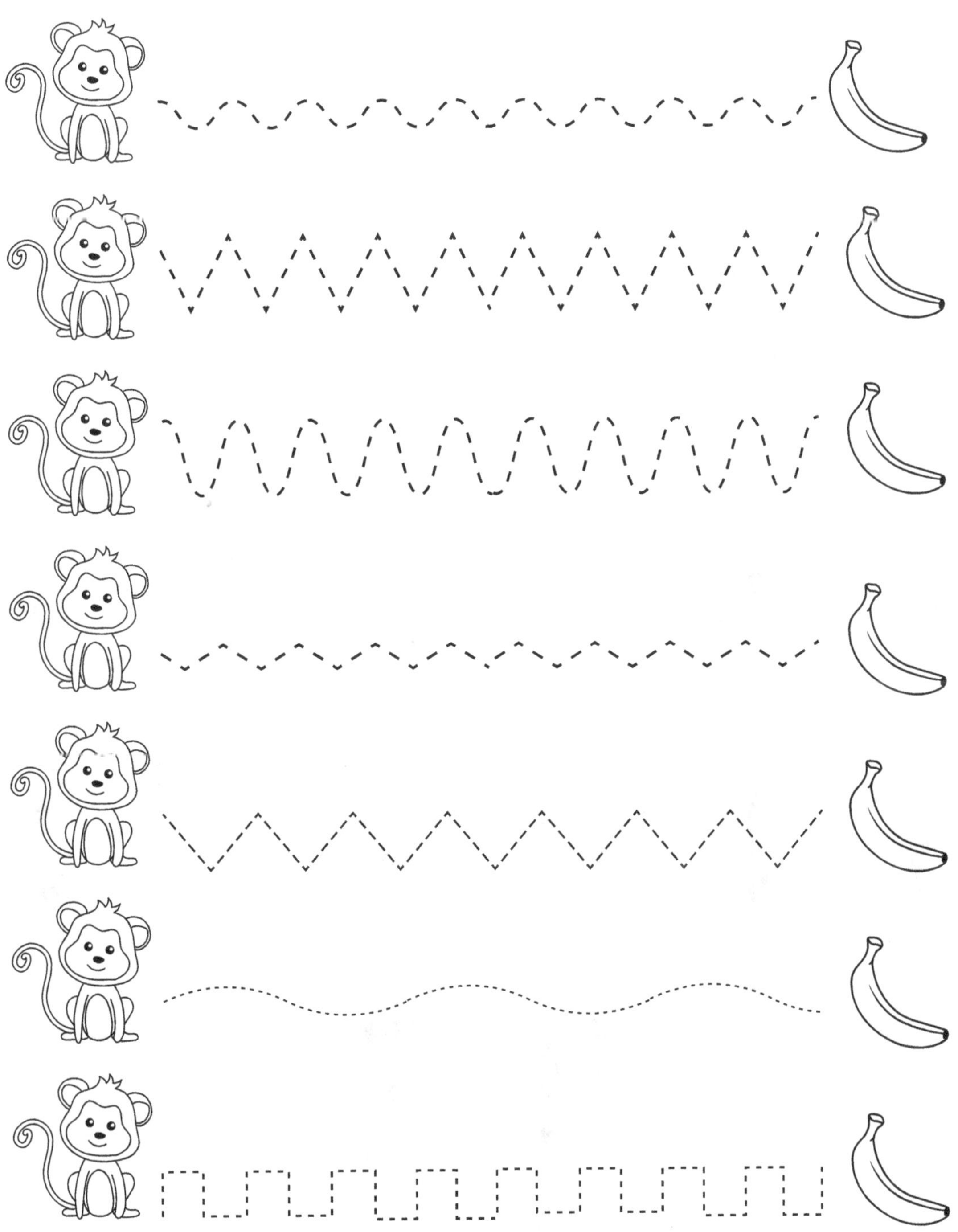

LET'S LEARN
Uppercase Letters

A B C D E F

G H I J K L

M N O P Q R

S T U V W X

Y Z

LET'S LEARN

Lowercase Letters

a b c d e f

g h i j k l

m n o p q r

s t u v w x

y z

LET'S LEARN
The Letters

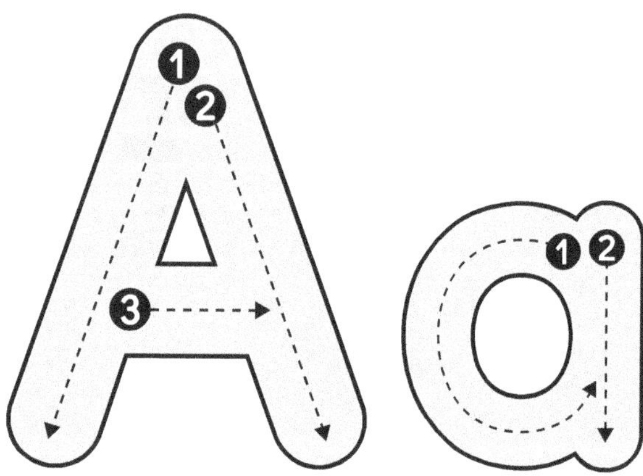

Trace the uppercase letter.

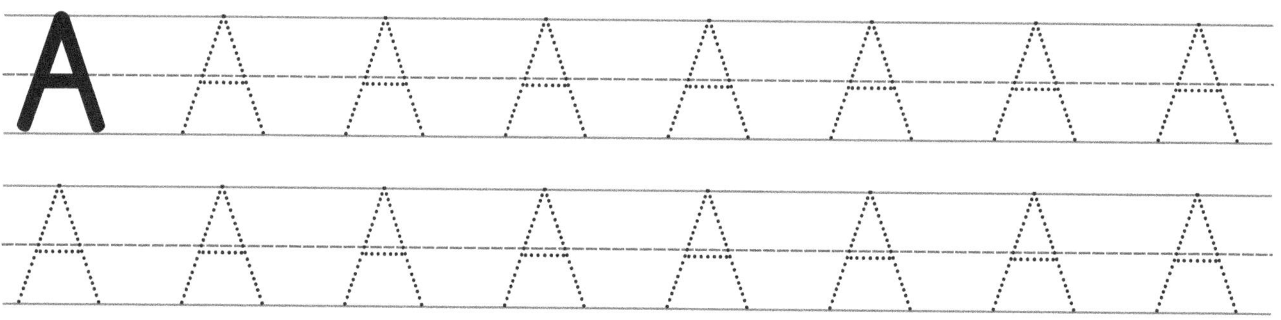

A

Trace the lowercase letter.

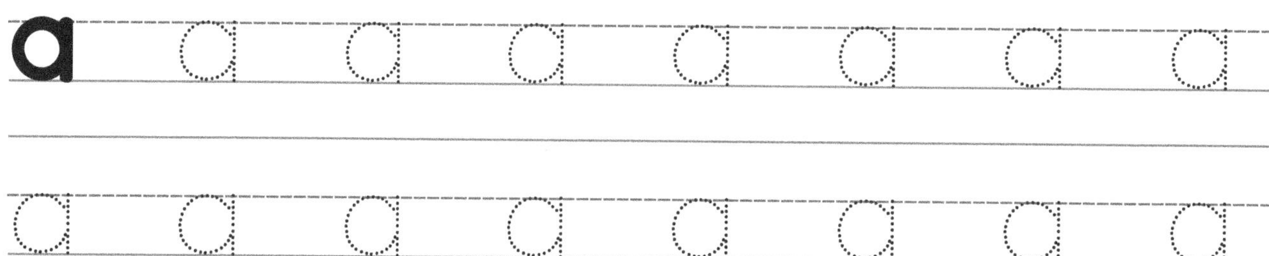

a

A	B	C	D	E	F	G	H	I	J	K	L	M	N	O	P	Q	R	S	T	U	V	W	X	Y	Z

Write the uppercase letter.

A

Write the lowercase letter.

a

Trace the words that begin with letter a.

angel   angel   angel

axe   axe   axe

ant   ant   ant

A B C D E F G H I J K L M N O P Q R S T U V W X Y Z

Write the letter a on each acorn.

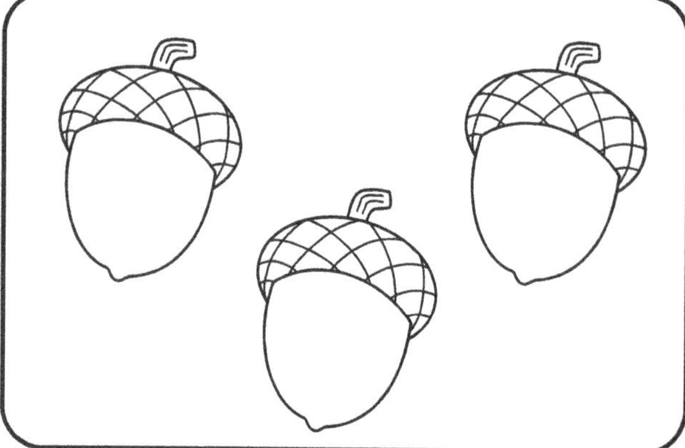

Color the picture.

Apple

Find and color the letter A.

Circle the first letter for each picture.

P A T

F C R

D C A

A B C D E F G H I J K L M N O P Q R S T U V W X Y Z

LET'S LEARN
The Letters

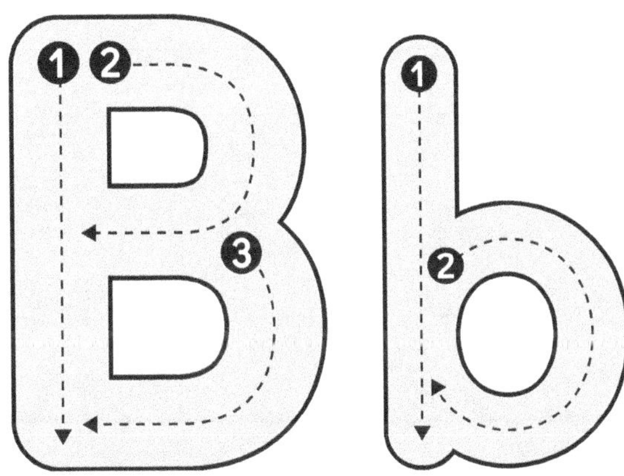

Trace the uppercase letter.

B B B B B B B B B B

B B B B B B B B B

Trace the lowercase letter.

b b b b b b b b

b b b b b b b

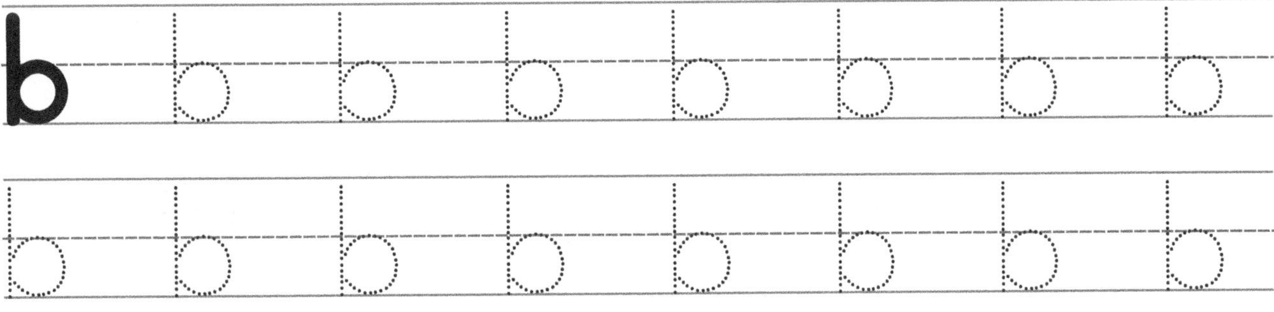

Write the uppercase letter.

B

Write the lowercase letter.

b

Trace the words that begin with letter b.

book   book   book

bell   bell   bell

bee   bee   bee

| A | B | C | D | E | F | G | H | I | J | K | L | M | N | O | P | Q | R | S | T | U | V | W | X | Y | Z |

Write the letter b on each bell.

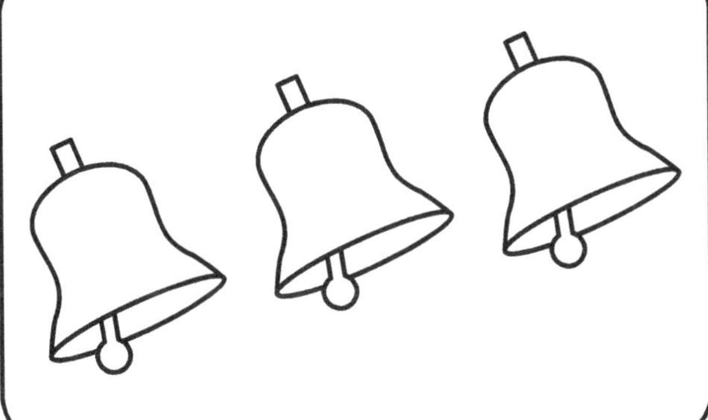

Find and color the letter B.

Color the picture.

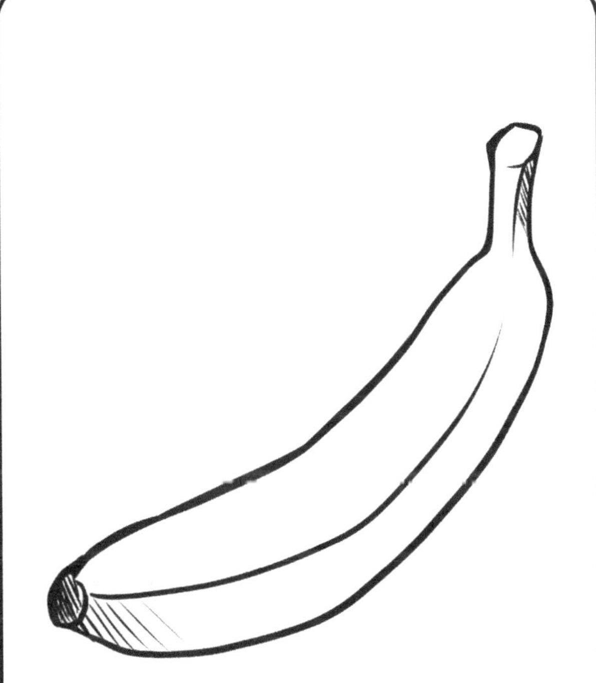

Banana

Circle the first letter for each picture.

B E I

M B A

D K H

| A | B | C | D | E | F | G | H | I | J | K | L | M | N | O | P | Q | R | S | T | U | V | W | X | Y | Z |

LET'S LEARN
The Letters

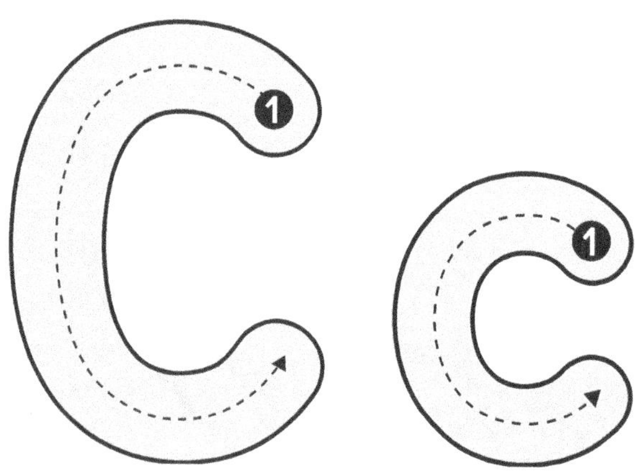

Trace the uppercase letter.

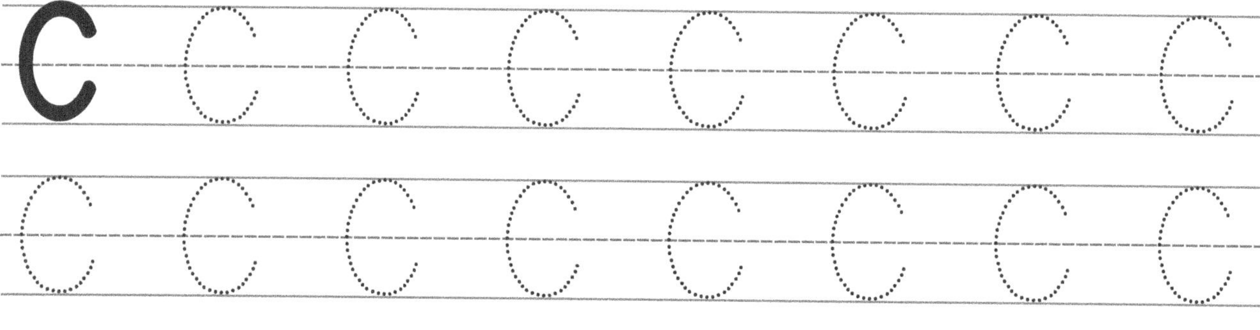

Trace the lowercase letter.

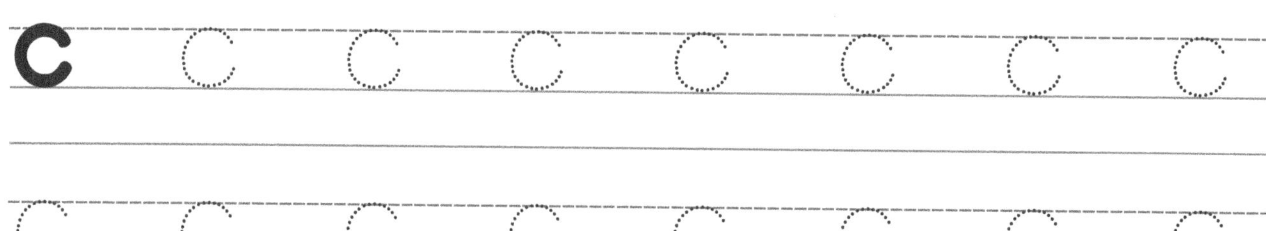

A	B	C	D	E	F	G	H	I	J	K	L	M	N	O	P	Q	R	S	T	U	V	W	X	Y	Z

Write the uppercase letter.

C

Write the lowercase letter.

c

Trace the words that begin with letter c.

corn   corn   corn

car   car   car

cow   cow   cow

| A | B | C | D | E | F | G | H | I | J | K | L | M | N | O | P | Q | R | S | T | U | V | W | X | Y | Z |

Write the letter c on each cup.

Color the picture.

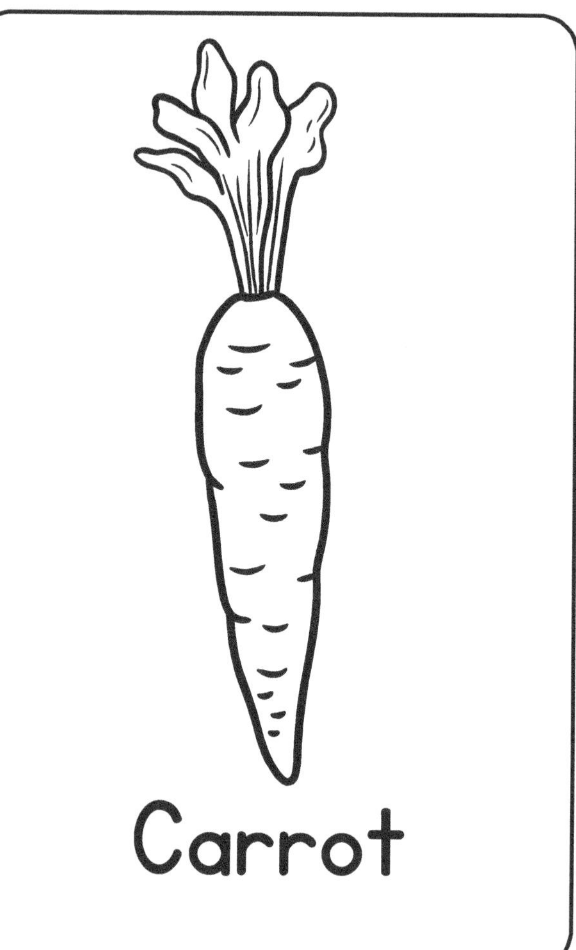

Carrot

Find and color the letter C.

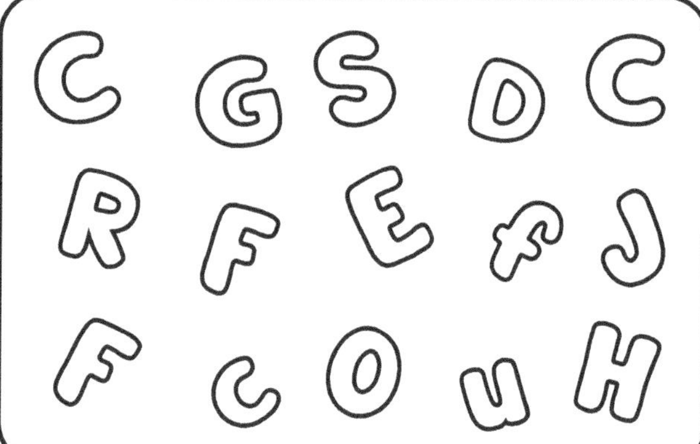

Circle the first letter for each picture.

C T R

C B C

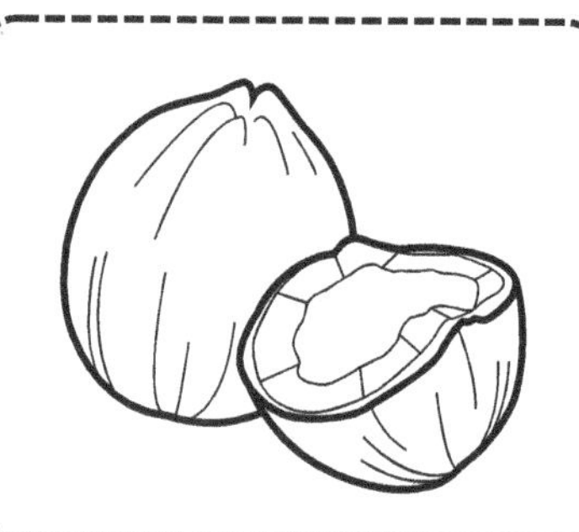

C A T

A B C D E F G H I J K L M N O P Q R S T U V W X Y Z

LET'S LEARN
The Letters

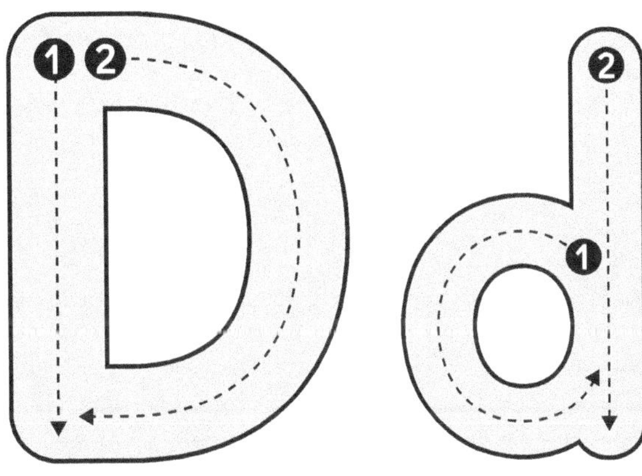

Trace the uppercase letter.

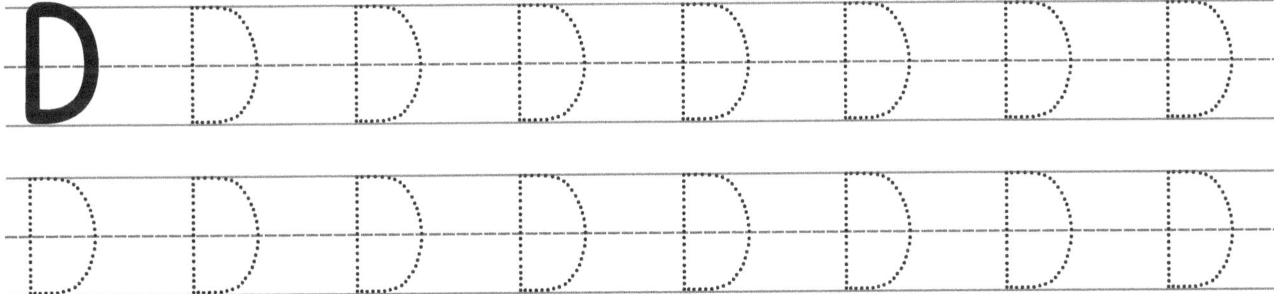

D

Trace the lowercase letter.

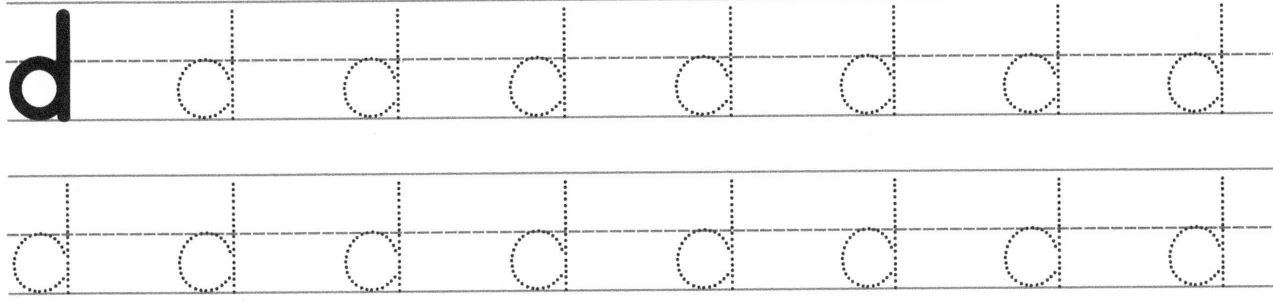

d

A B C D E F G H I J K L M N O P Q R S T U V W X Y Z

Write the uppercase letter.

D

Write the lowercase letter.

d

Trace the words that begin with letter d.

door   door   door

doll   doll   doll

duck   duck   duck

| A | B | C | D | E | F | G | H | I | J | K | L | M | N | O | P | Q | R | S | T | U | V | W | X | Y | Z |

Write the letter d on each duck.

Find and color the letter D.

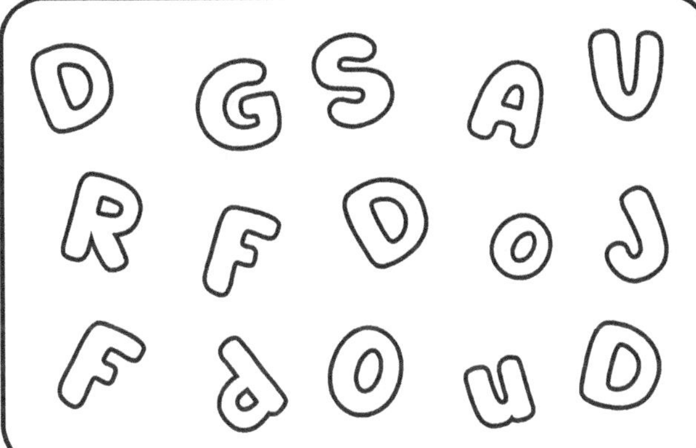

Color the picture.

Dress

Circle the first letter for each picture.

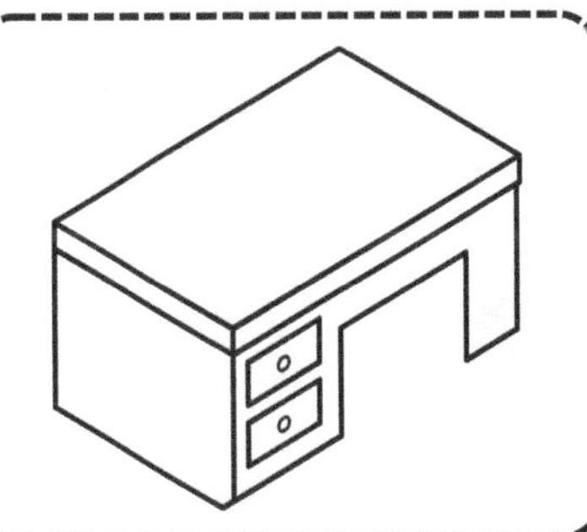

| B | D | R | | C | B | A | | M | E | D |

LET'S LEARN
The Letters

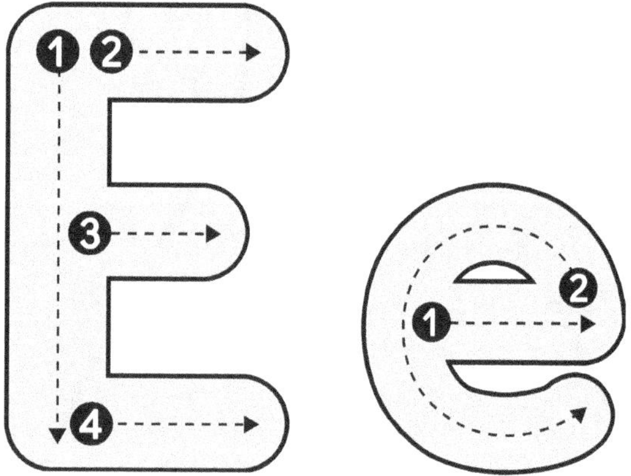

Trace the uppercase letter.

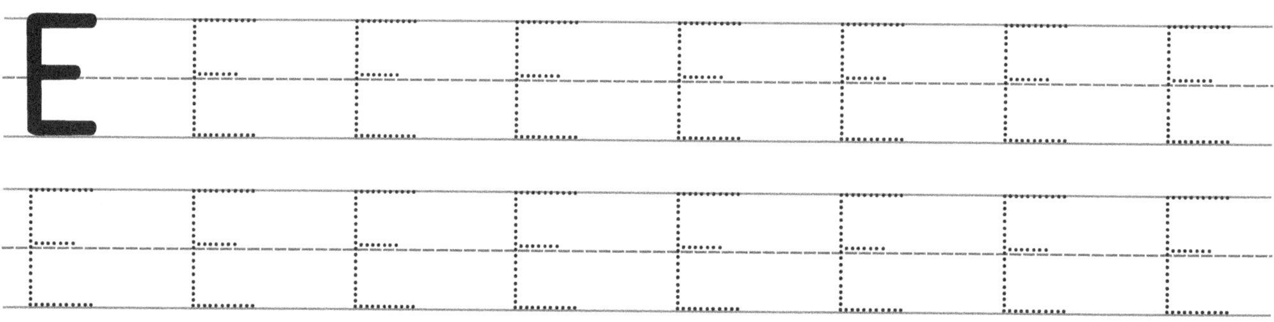

Trace the lowercase letter.

A	B	C	D	E	F	G	H	I	J	K	L	M	N	O	P	Q	R	S	T	U	V	W	X	Y	Z

Write the uppercase letter.

E

Write the lowercase letter.

e

Trace the words that begin with letter e.

eagle eagle eagle

egg egg egg

elf elf elf

| A | B | C | D | E | F | G | H | I | J | K | L | M | N | O | P | Q | R | S | T | U | V | W | X | Y | Z |

Write the letter e on each egg.

Color the picture.

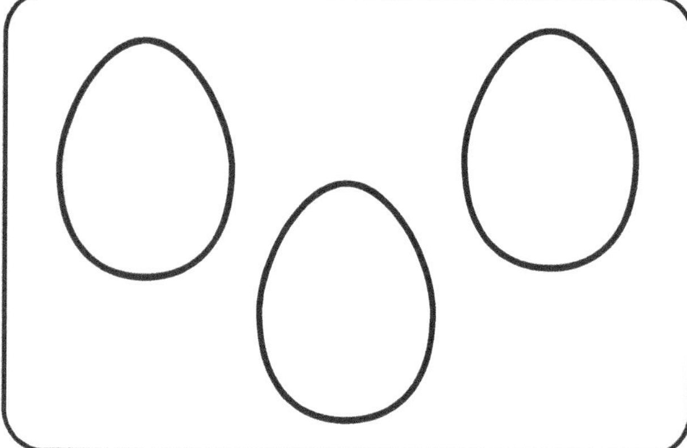

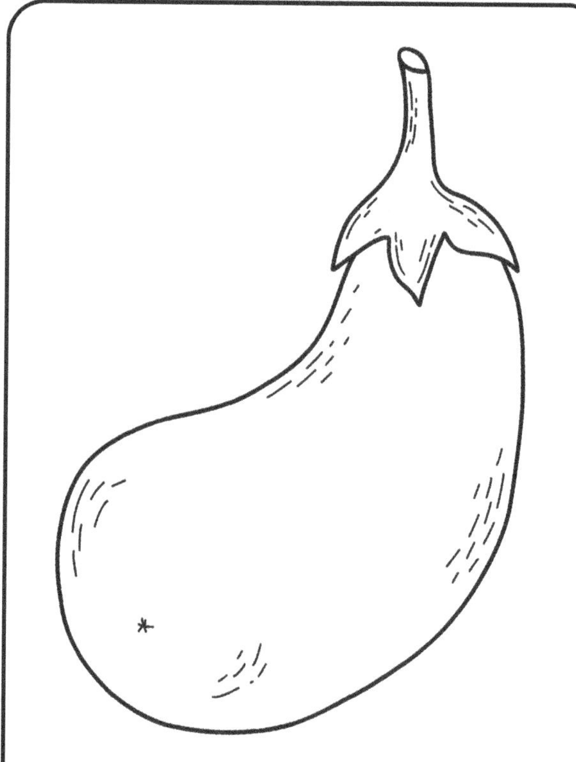

Eggplant

Find and color the letter E.

Circle the first letter for each picture.

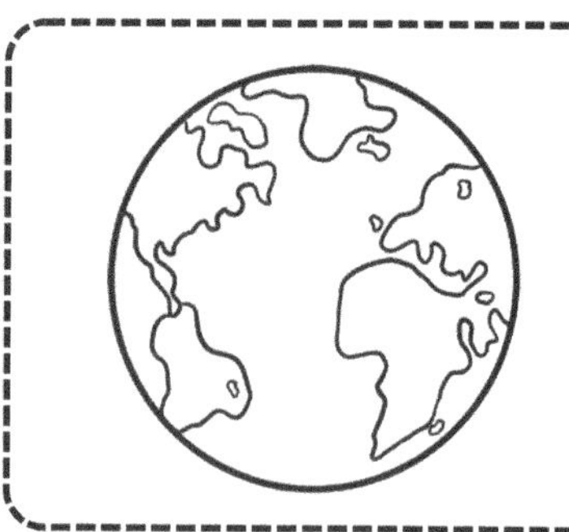

| B | D | R | | C | B | A | | M | E | D |

A B C D **E** F G H I J K L M N O P Q R S T U V W X Y Z

LET'S LEARN
The Letters

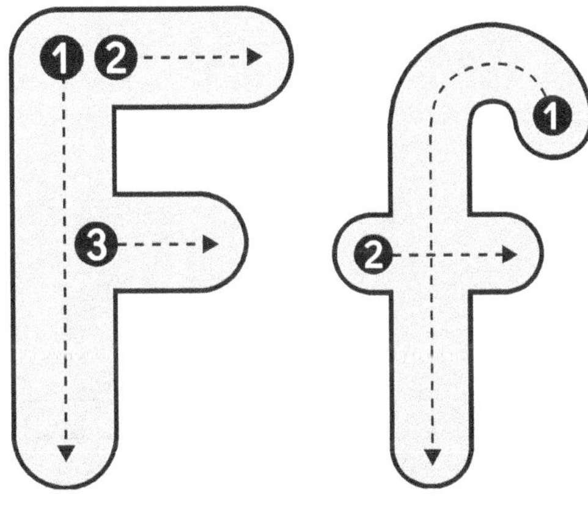

Trace the uppercase letter.

F

Trace the lowercase letter.

f

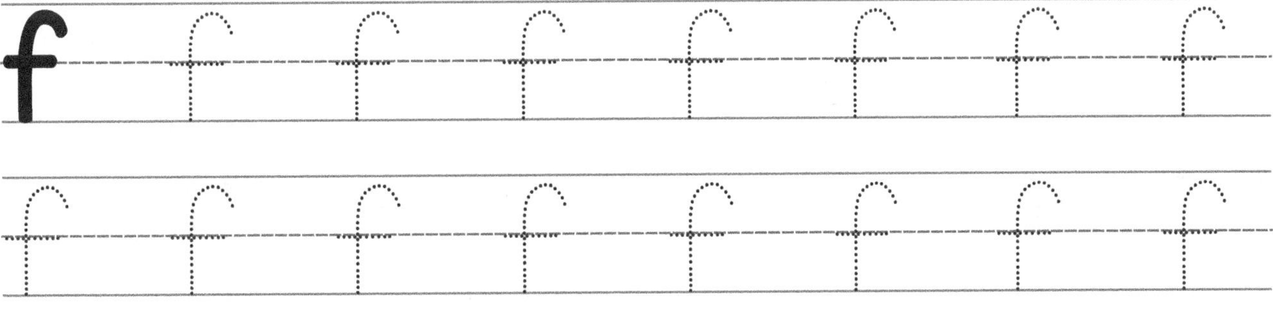

24

Write the uppercase letter.

F

Write the lowercase letter.

f

Trace the words that begin with letter f.

frog   frog   frog

flag   flag   flag

fire   fire   fire

| A | B | C | D | E | F | G | H | I | J | K | L | M | N | O | P | Q | R | S | T | U | V | W | X | Y | Z |

Write the letter f on each fish.

Color the picture.

Flower

Find and color the letter F.

Circle the first letter for each picture.

U	T	B

N	F	B

F	O	K

A B C D E **F** G H I J K L M N O P Q R S T U V W X Y Z

LET'S LEARN
The Letters

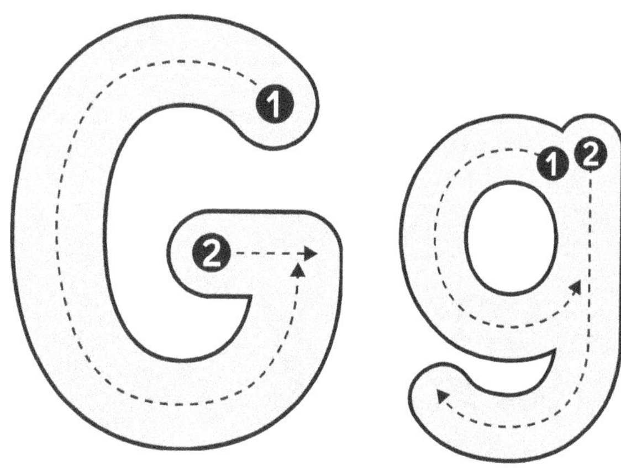

Trace the uppercase letter.

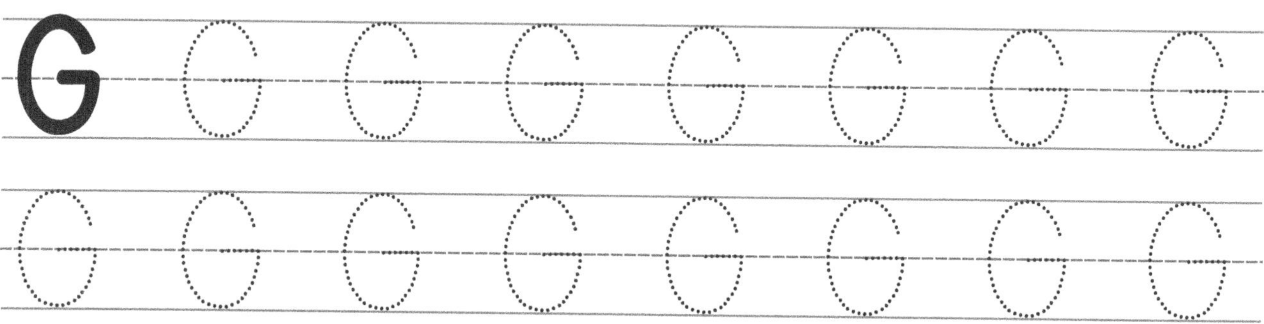

Trace the lowercase letter.

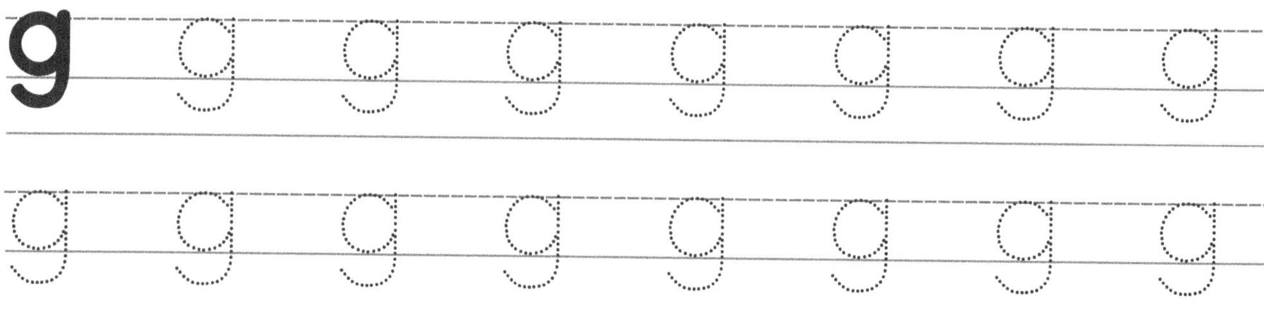

A	B	C	D	E	F	G	H	I	J	K	L	M	N	O	P	Q	R	S	T	U	V	W	X	Y	Z

Write the uppercase letter.

G

Write the lowercase letter.

g

Trace the words that begin with letter g.

glass glass glass

gift gift gift

goat goat goat

| A | B | C | D | E | F | G | H | I | J | K | L | M | N | O | P | Q | R | S | T | U | V | W | X | Y | Z |

Write the letter g on each gift.

Color the picture.

Grapes

Find and color the letter G.

Circle the first letter for each picture.

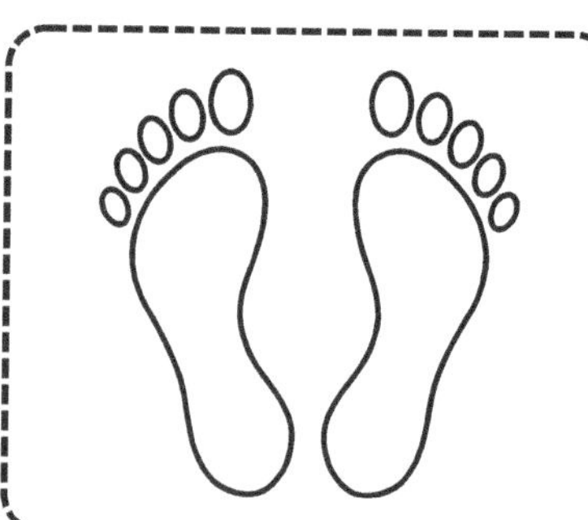

| D | O | G | | G | T | R | | A | F | C |

A B C D E F **G** H I J K L M N O P Q R S T U V W X Y Z

LET'S LEARN
The Letters

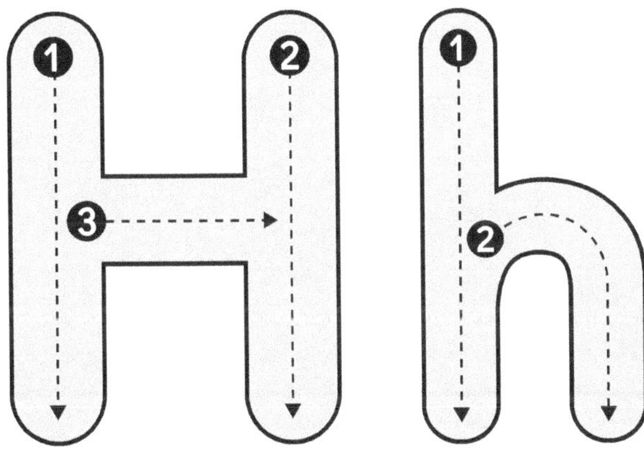

Trace the uppercase letter.

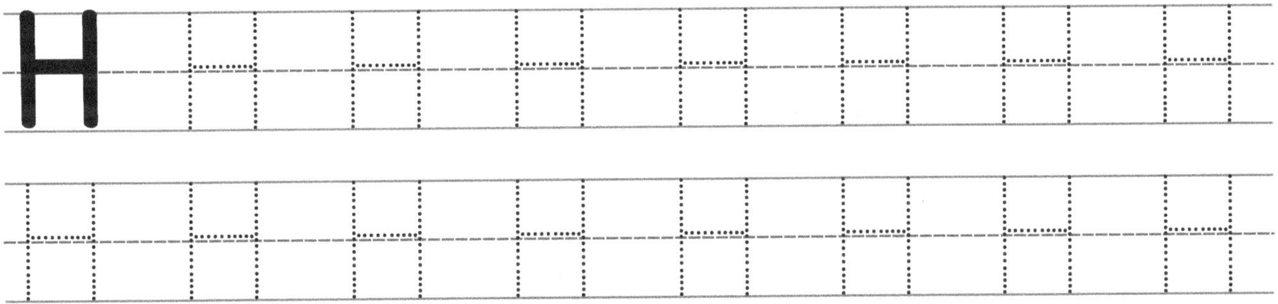

Trace the lowercase letter.

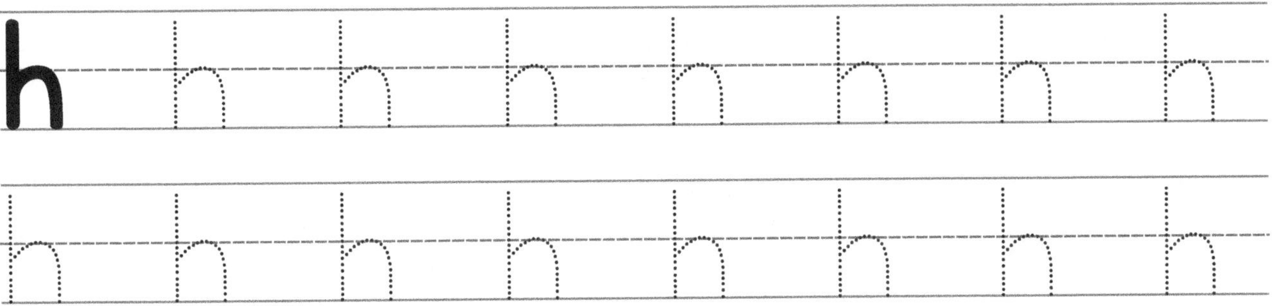

A	B	C	D	E	F	G	H	I	J	K	L	M	N	O	P	Q	R	S	T	U	V	W	X	Y	Z

Write the uppercase letter.

H

Write the lowercase letter.

h

Trace the words that begin with letter h.

hand   hand   hand

hat   hat   hat

hen   hen   hen

Write the letter h on each heart.

Color the picture.

House

Find and color the letter H.

Circle the first letter for each picture.

O H N

A V D

R S H

A B C D E F G H I J K L M N O P Q R S T U V W X Y Z

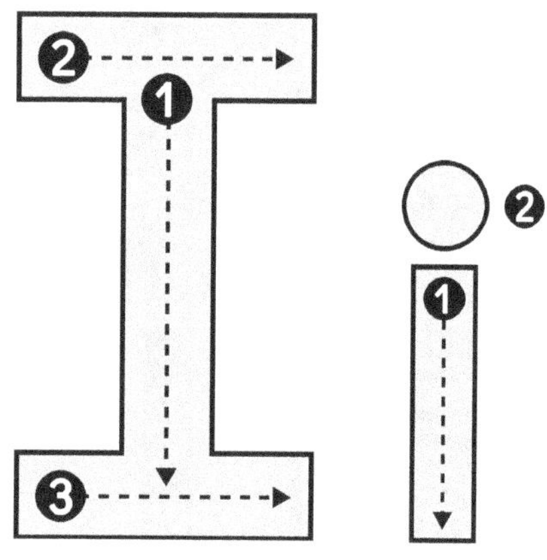

Trace the uppercase letter.

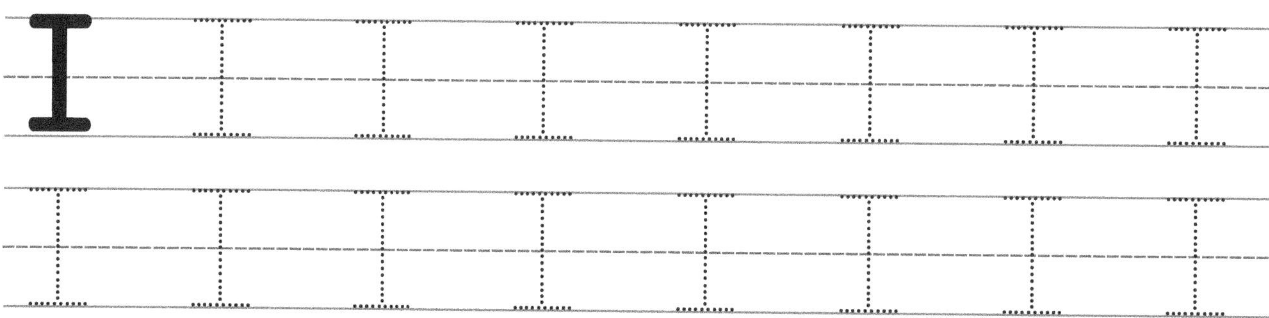

Trace the lowercase letter.

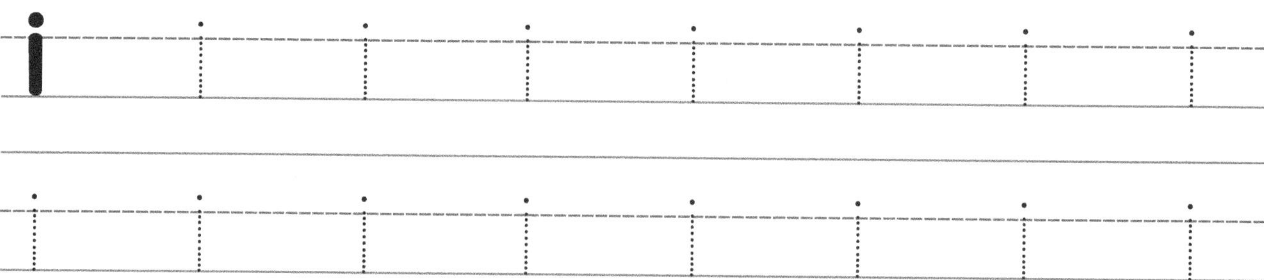

Write the uppercase letter.

I

Write the lowercase letter.

i

Trace the words that begin with letter i.

igloo   igloo   igloo

ice   ice   ice

iron   iron   iron

| A | B | C | D | E | F | G | H | I | J | K | L | M | N | O | P | Q | R | S | T | U | V | W | X | Y | Z |

Write the letter i on each ice cream.

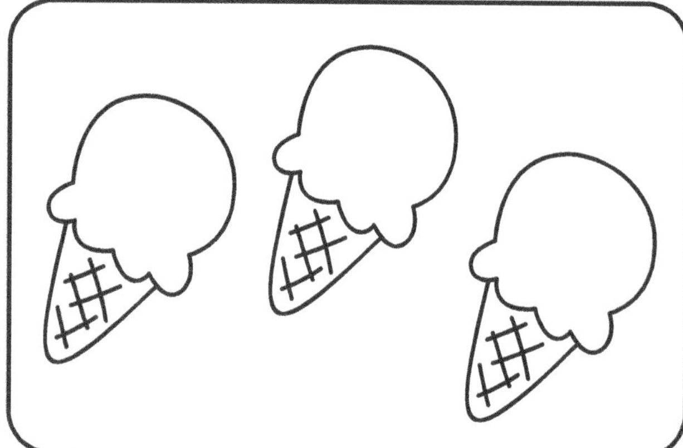

Find and color the letter I.

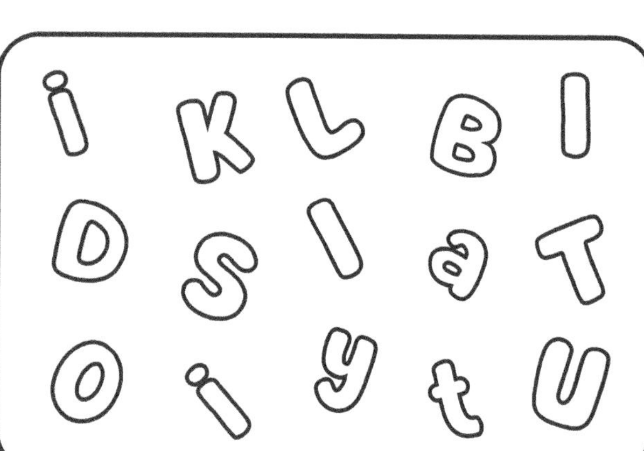

Color the picture.

Circle the first letter for each picture.

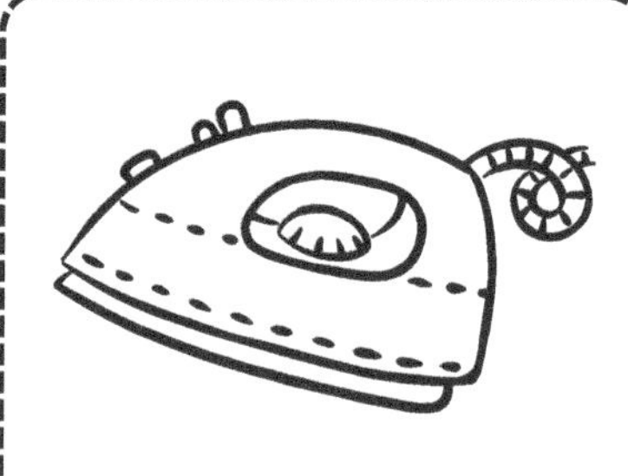

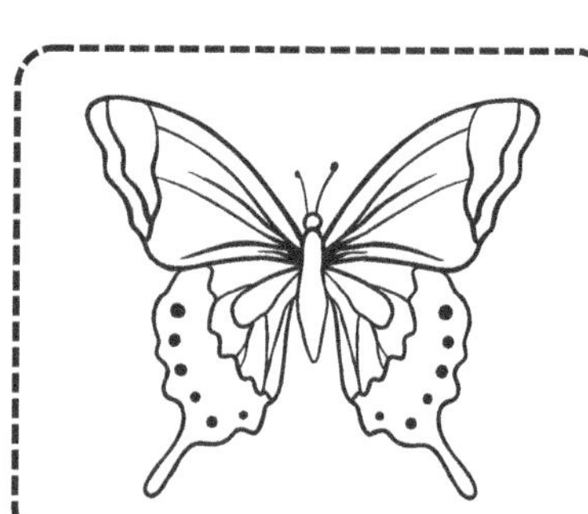

| I | A | B | | D | I | F | | H | A | B |

LET'S LEARN
The Letters

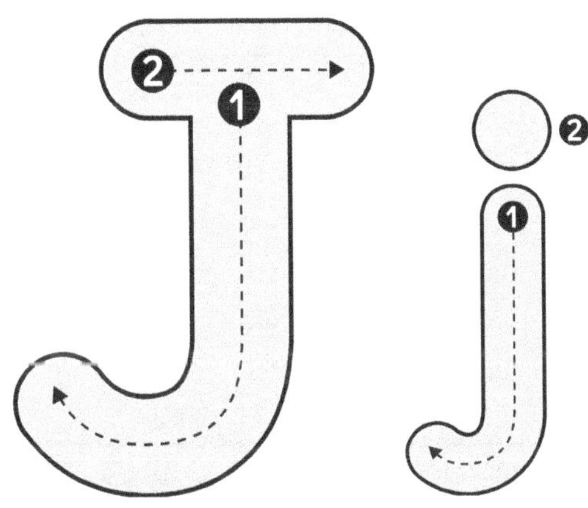

Trace the uppercase letter.

J

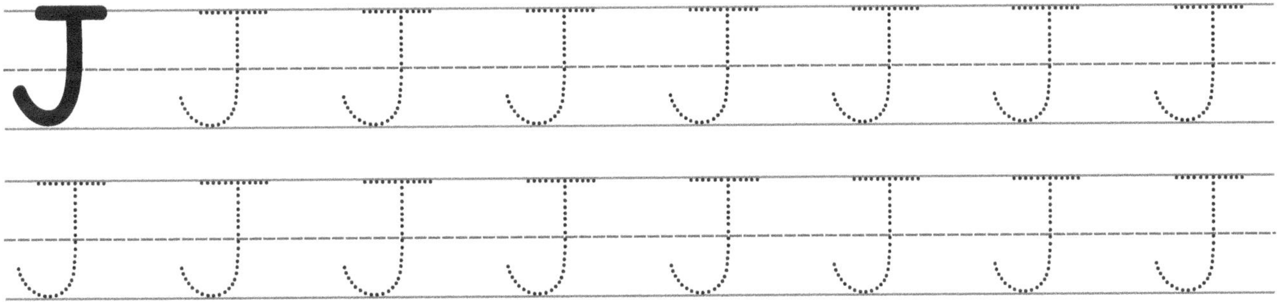

Trace the lowercase letter.

j

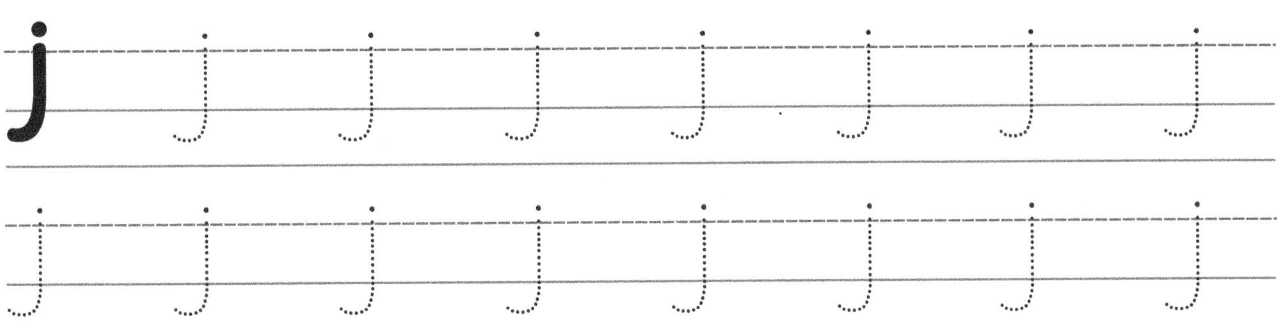

| A | B | C | D | E | F | G | H | I | J | K | L | M | N | O | P | Q | R | S | T | U | V | W | X | Y | Z |

Write the uppercase letter.

J

Write the lowercase letter.

j

Trace the words that begin with letter j.

juice   juice   juice

jug   jug   jug

jeans   jeans   jeans

Write the letter j on each jar.

Color the picture.

Jacket

Find and color the letter J.

Circle the first letter for each picture.

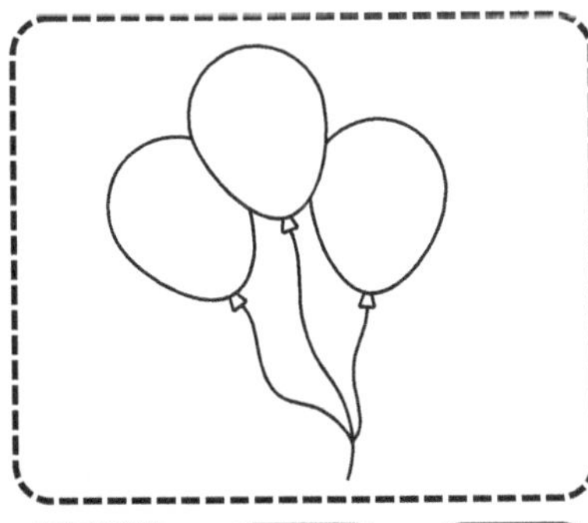

N	B	A

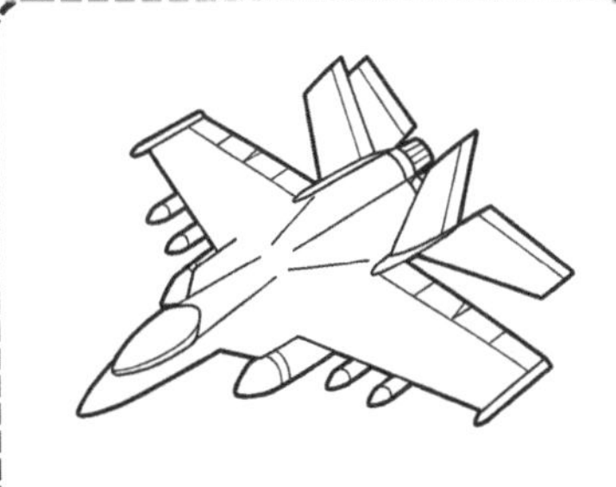

J	R	C

F	G	J

A B C D E F G H I **J** K L M N O P Q R S T U V W X Y Z

LET'S LEARN
The Letters

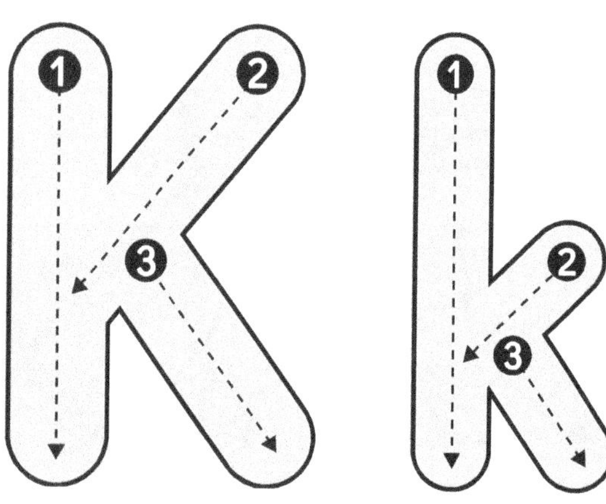

Trace the uppercase letter.

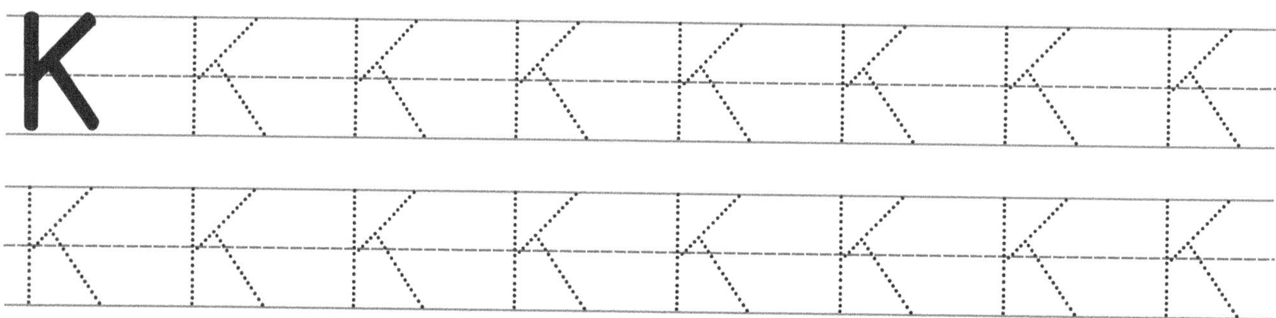

Trace the lowercase letter.

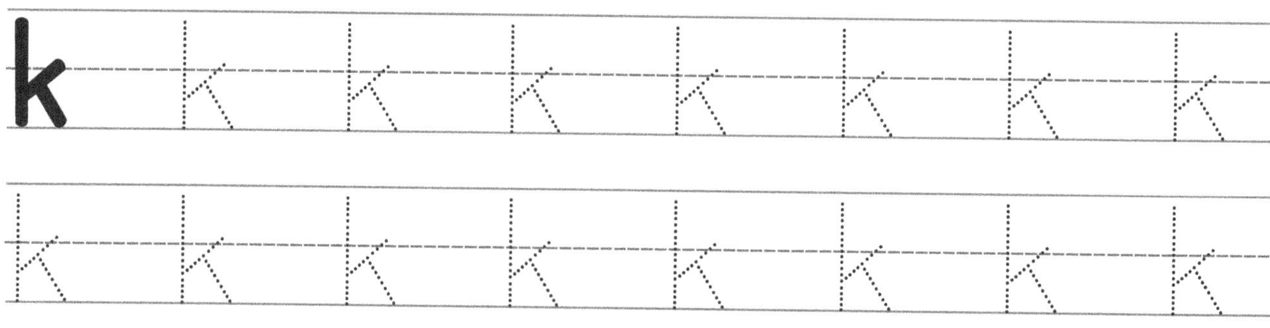

Write the uppercase letter.

K

Write the lowercase letter.

k

Trace the words that begin with letter k.

knife knife knife

key key key

king king king

A	B	C	D	E	F	G	H	I	J	K	L	M	N	O	P	Q	R	S	T	U	V	W	X	Y	Z

Write the letter k on each kettle.

Color the picture.

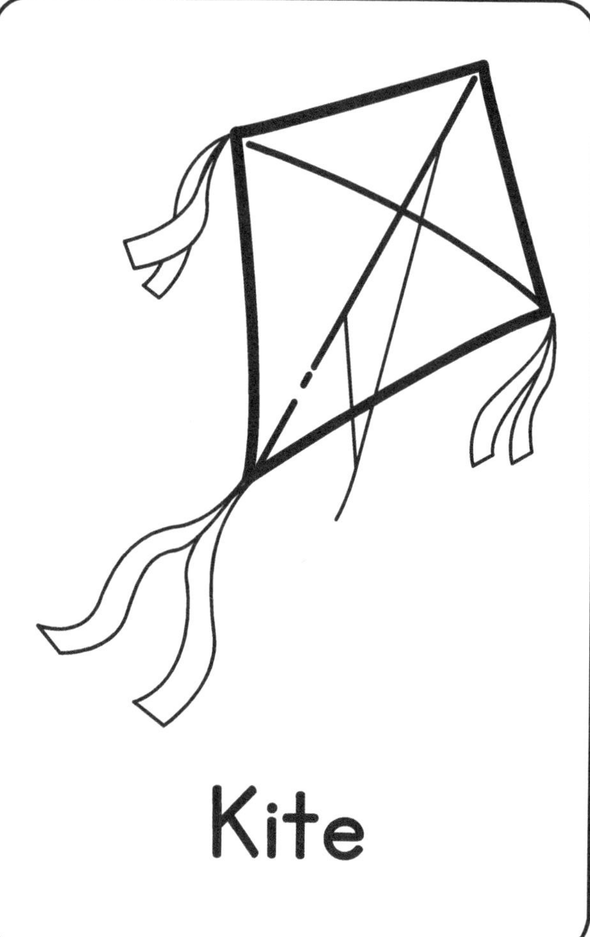

Kite

Find and color the letter K.

Circle the first letter for each picture.

| K | A | F |

| B | A | C |

| L | N | K |

A B C D E F G H I J K L M N O P Q R S T U V W X Y Z

LET'S LEARN
The Letters

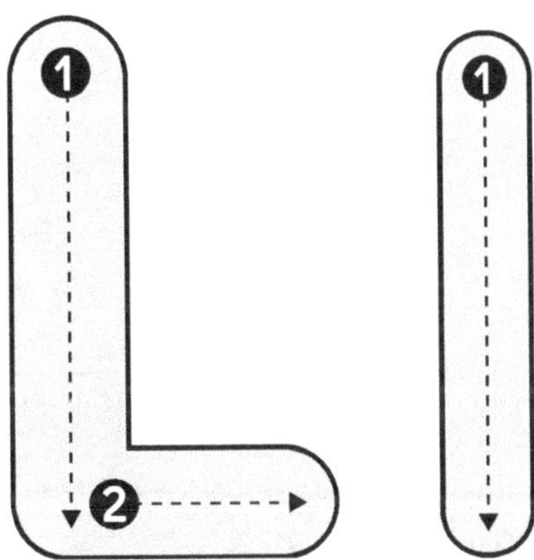

Trace the uppercase letter.

Trace the lowercase letter.

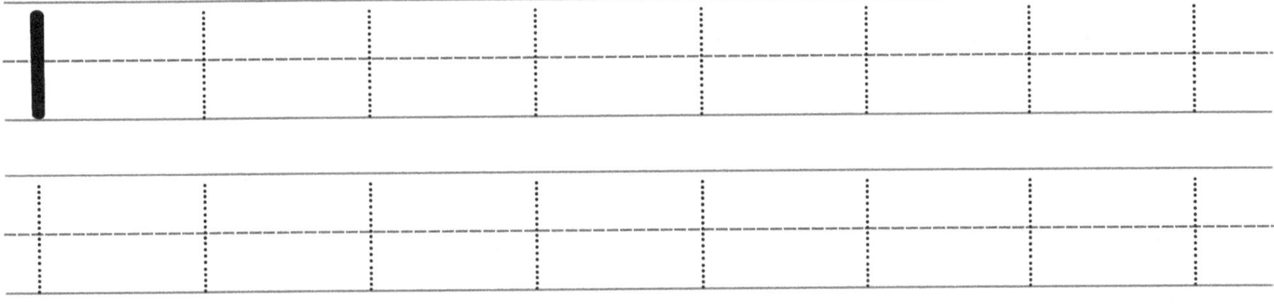

42

Write the uppercase letter.

L

Write the lowercase letter.

l

Trace the words that begin with letter l.

lamp lamp lamp

leaf leaf leaf

lip lip lip

| A | B | C | D | E | F | G | H | I | J | K | L | M | N | O | P | Q | R | S | T | U | V | W | X | Y | Z |

Write the letter l on each lemon.

Find and color the letter L.

Color the picture.

Ladybug

Circle the first letter for each picture.

C   I   D

L   O   A

A   L   B

A B C D E F G H I J K L M N O P Q R S T U V W X Y Z

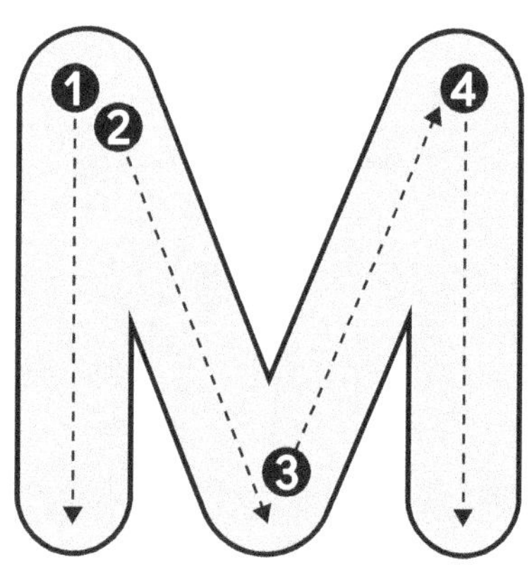

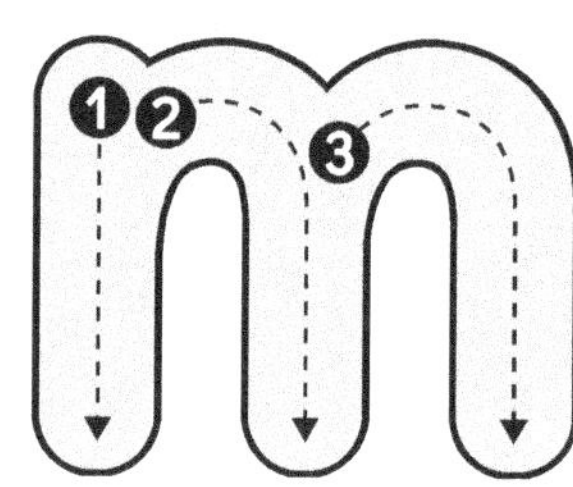

Trace the uppercase letter.

M

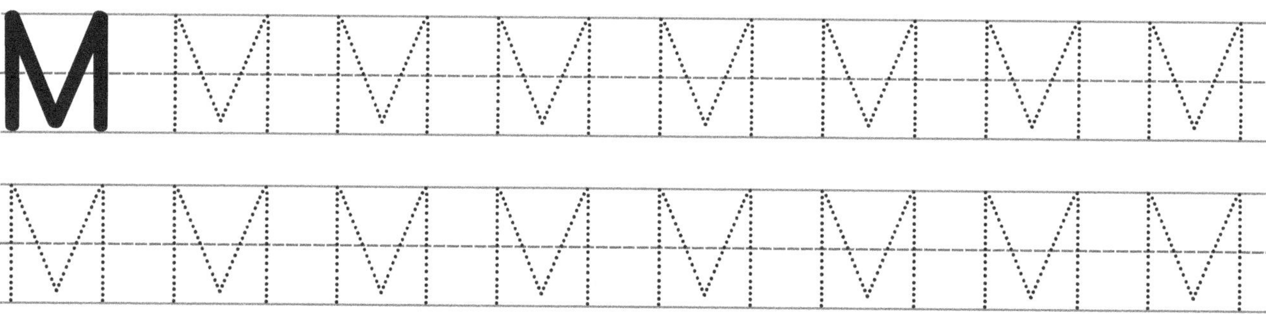

Trace the lowercase letter.

m

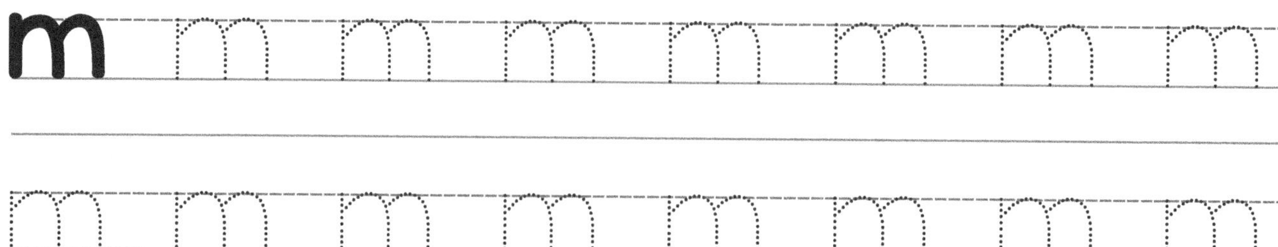

A	B	C	D	E	F	G	H	I	J	K	L	M	N	O	P	Q	R	S	T	U	V	W	X	Y	Z

Write the uppercase letter.

M

Write the lowercase letter.

m

Trace the words that begin with letter m.

meat   meat   meat

man   man   man

mug   mug   mug

| A | B | C | D | E | F | G | H | I | J | K | L | M | N | O | P | Q | R | S | T | U | V | W | X | Y | Z |

Write the letter m on each moon.

Color the picture.

Mermaid

Find and color the letter M.

Circle the first letter for each picture.

D O M

J M F

B R C

| A | B | C | D | E | F | G | H | I | J | K | L | M | N | O | P | Q | R | S | T | U | V | W | X | Y | Z |

LET'S LEARN
The Letters

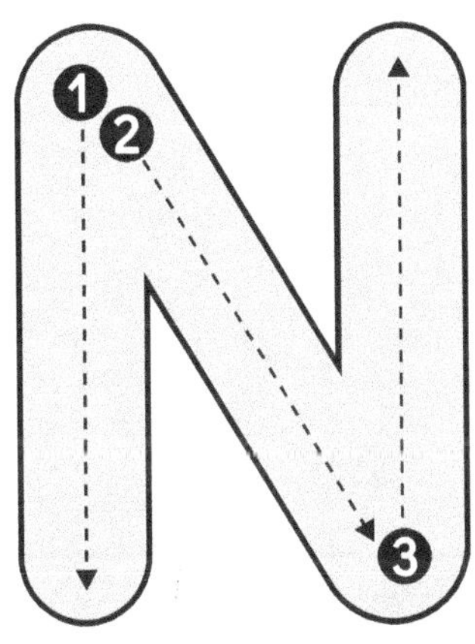

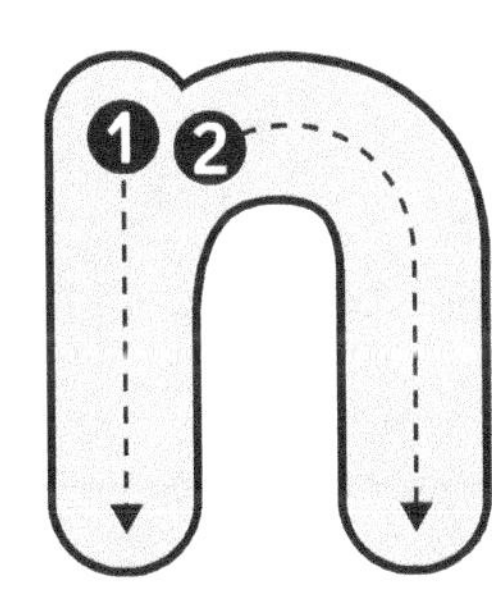

Trace the uppercase letter.

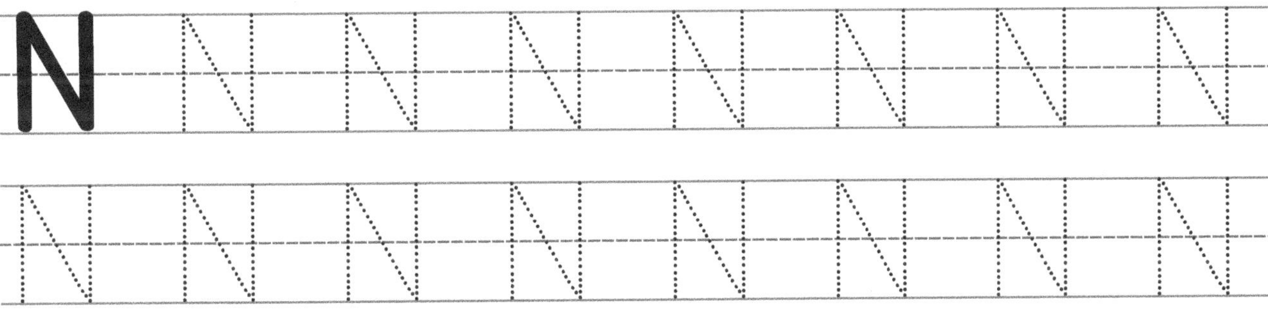

Trace the lowercase letter.

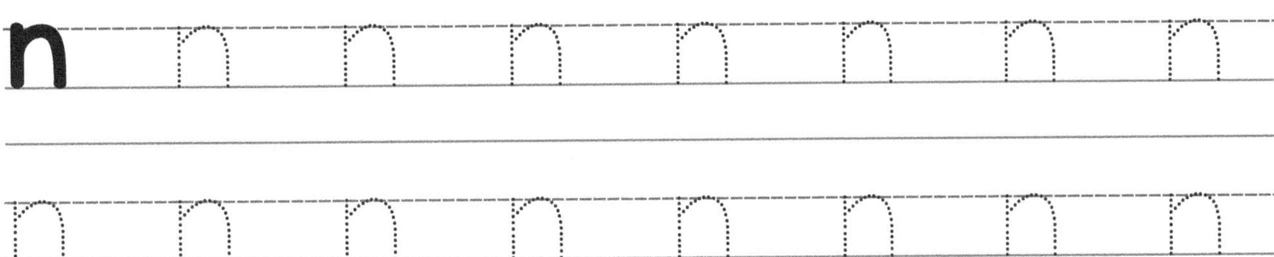

| A | B | C | D | E | F | G | H | I | J | K | L | M | N | O | P | Q | R | S | T | U | V | W | X | Y | Z |

Write the uppercase letter.

N

Write the lowercase letter.

n

Trace the words that begin with letter n.

nurse nurse nurse

nose nose nose

nail nail nail

| A | B | C | D | E | F | G | H | I | J | K | L | M | N | O | P | Q | R | S | T | U | V | W | X | Y | Z |

Write the letter n on each nose.

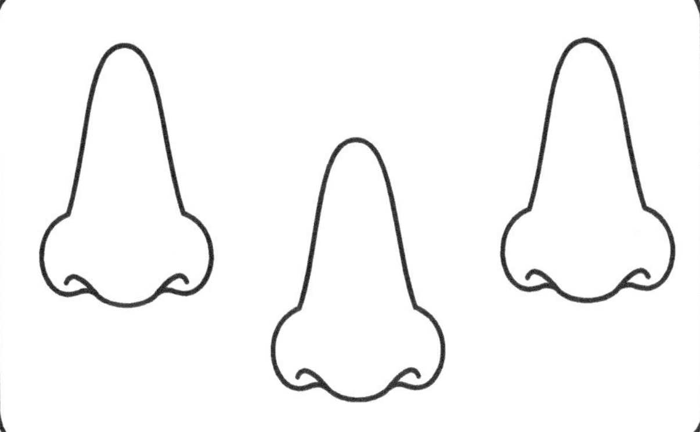

Color the picture.

Nest

Find and color the letter N.

Circle the first letter for each picture.

M	A	B

E	N	D

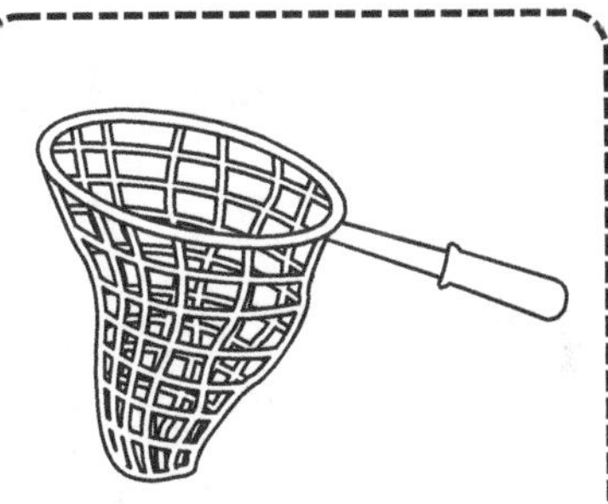

F	T	N

A	B	C	D	E	F	G	H	I	J	K	L	M	N	O	P	Q	R	S	T	U	V	W	X	Y	Z

LET'S LEARN
The Letters

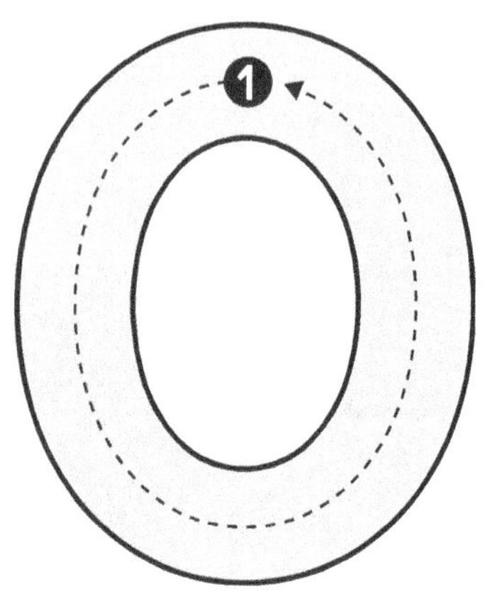

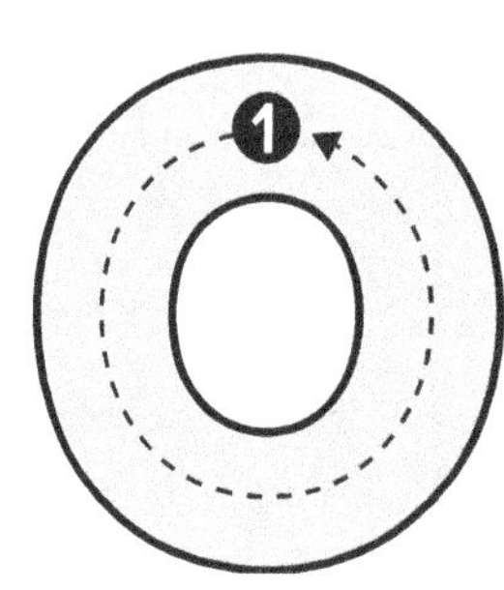

Trace the uppercase letter.

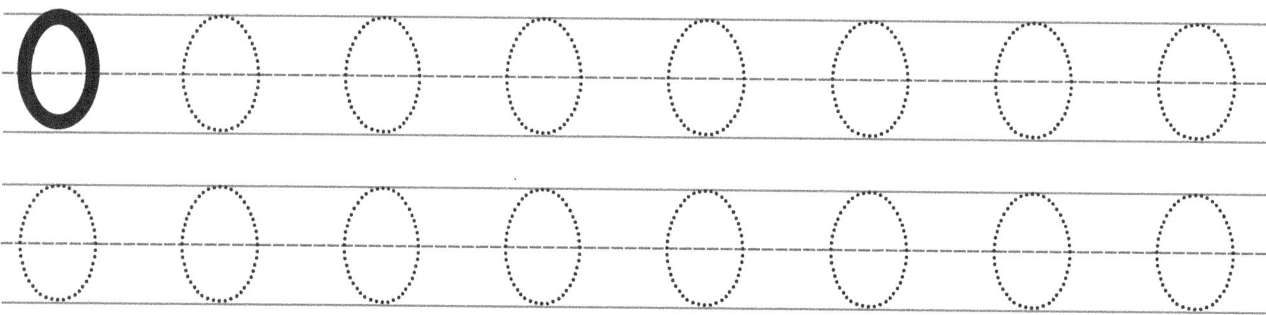

Trace the lowercase letter.

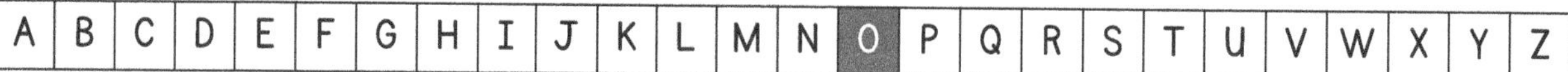

A	B	C	D	E	F	G	H	I	J	K	L	M	N	O	P	Q	R	S	T	U	V	W	X	Y	Z

Write the uppercase letter.

O

Write the lowercase letter.

o

Trace the words that begin with letter o.

oven   oven   oven

oval   oval   oval

oil   oil   oil

Write the letter o on each orange.

Color the picture.

Octopus

Find and color the letter O.

Circle the first letter for each picture.

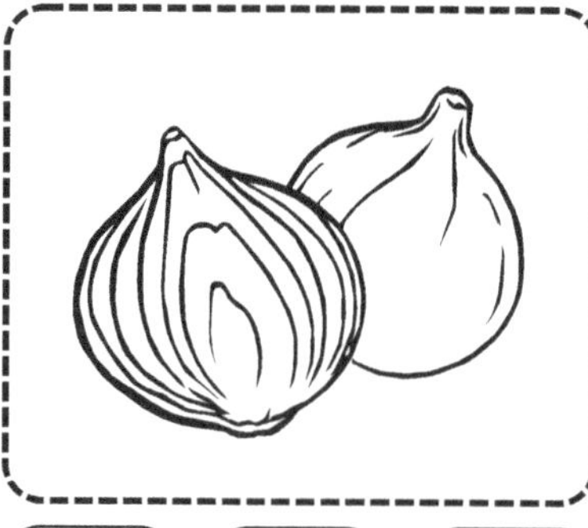

B　O　N   L　F　E   O　G　K

A B C D E F G H I J K L M N O P Q R S T U V W X Y Z

53

LET'S LEARN

The Letters

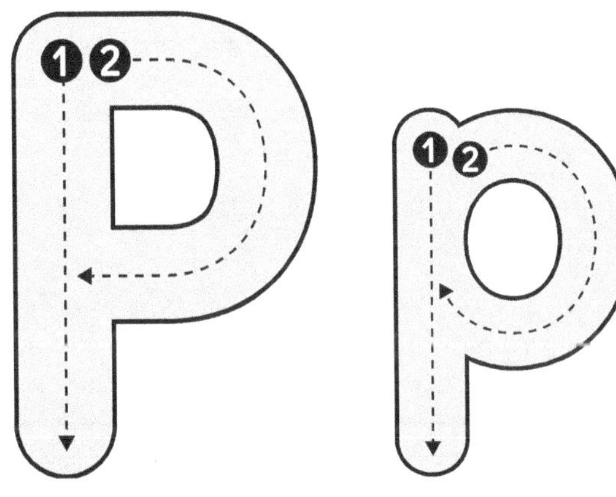

Trace the uppercase letter.

P P P P P P P P P

P P P P P P P P P

Trace the lowercase letter.

p p p p p p p p p

p p p p p p p p p

| A | B | C | D | E | F | G | H | I | J | K | L | M | N | O | P | Q | R | S | T | U | V | W | X | Y | Z |

Write the uppercase letter.

P

Write the lowercase letter.

p

Trace the words that begin with letter p.

pear   pear   pear

pan   pan   pan

park   park   park

| A | B | C | D | E | F | G | H | I | J | K | L | M | N | O | P | Q | R | S | T | U | V | W | X | Y | Z |

Write the letter p on each pumpkin.

Color the picture.

Pirate

Find and color the letter P.

Circle the first letter for each picture.

| U | N | P | | P | M | I | | A | C | B |

A B C D E F G H I J K L M N O **P** Q R S T U V W X Y Z

56

LET'S LEARN
The Letters

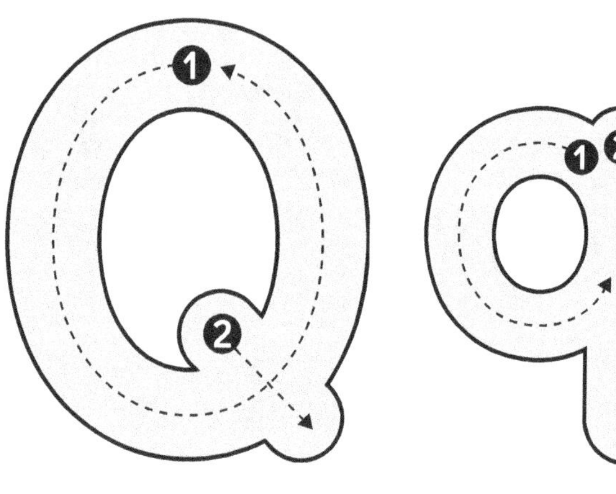

Trace the uppercase letter.

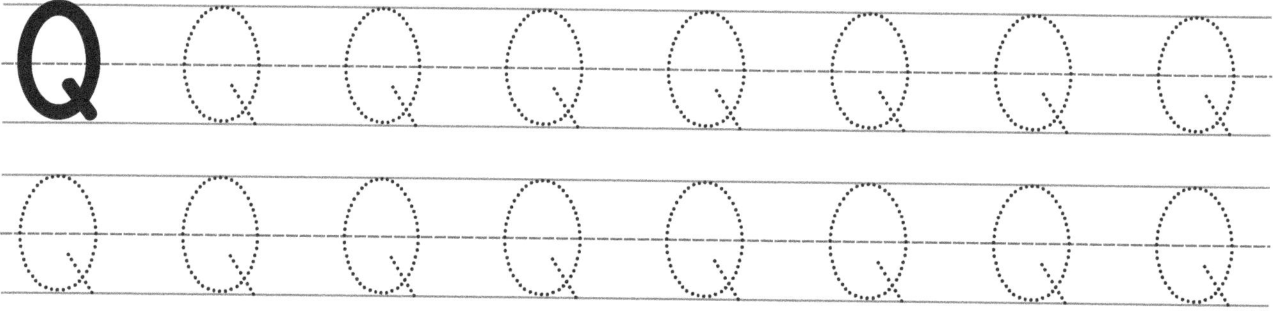

Trace the lowercase letter.

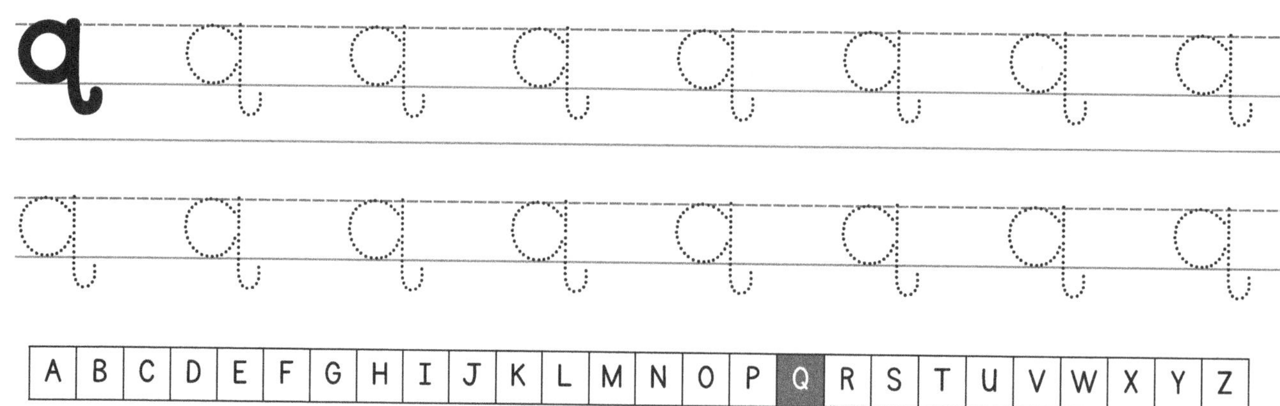

| A | B | C | D | E | F | G | H | I | J | K | L | M | N | O | P | Q | R | S | T | U | V | W | X | Y | Z |

Write the uppercase letter.

Q

Write the lowercase letter.

q

Trace the words that begin with letter q.

quiet quiet quiet

quilt quilt quilt

queen queen queen

A B C D E F G H I J K L M N O P Q R S T U V W X Y Z

Write the letter q on each quince.

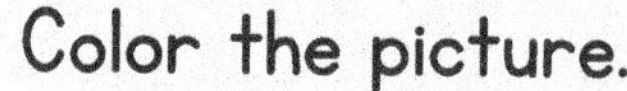

Color the picture.

Find and color the letter Q.

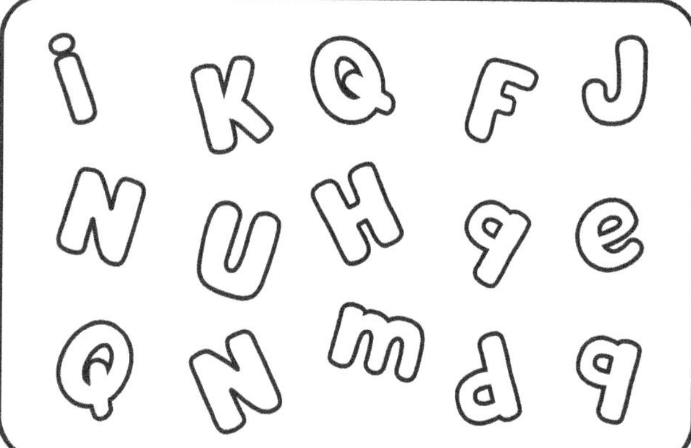

Quad

Circle the first letter for each picture.

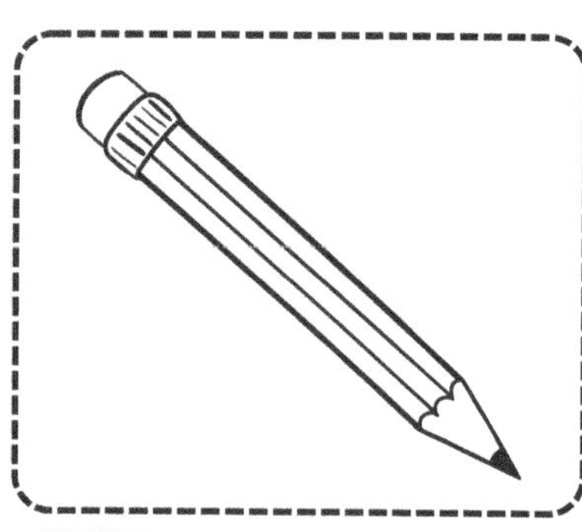

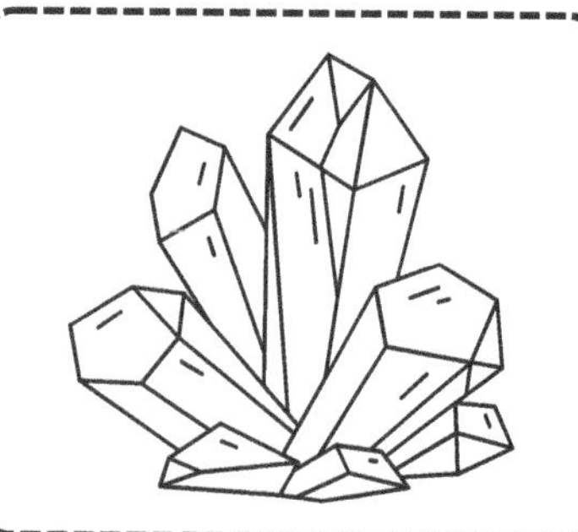

P	M	O

J	Q	K

B	U	Q

A	B	C	D	E	F	G	H	I	J	K	L	M	N	O	P	Q	R	S	T	U	V	W	X	Y	Z

LET'S LEARN
The Letters

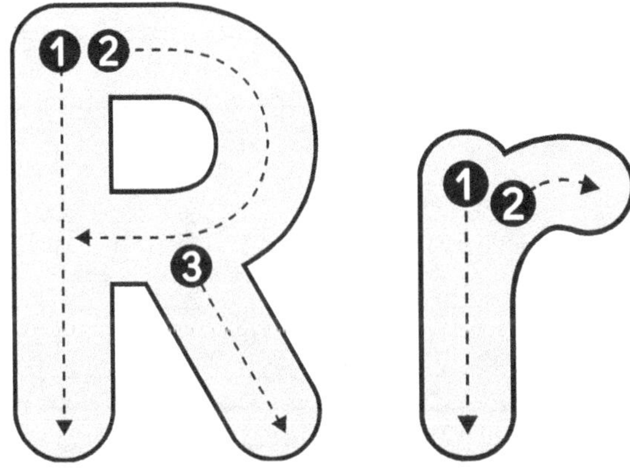

Trace the uppercase letter.

R R R R R R R R R

R R R R R R R R

Trace the lowercase letter.

r r r r r r r r r

r r r r r r r r

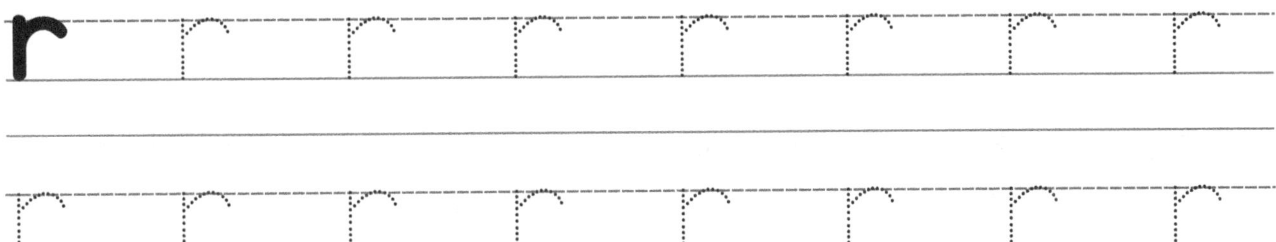

Write the uppercase letter.

R

Write the lowercase letter.

r

Trace the words that begin with letter r.

rice   rice   rice

ring   ring   ring

rose   rose   rose

| A | B | C | D | E | F | G | H | I | J | K | L | M | N | O | P | Q | R | S | T | U | V | W | X | Y | Z |

Write the letter r on each rocket.

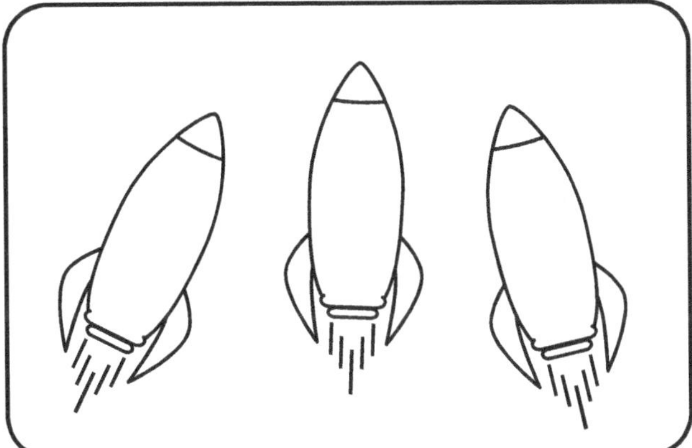

Find and color the letter R.

Color the picture.

Robot

Circle the first letter for each picture.

| R | B | O | | N | R | I | | M | H | B |

A B C D E F G H I J K L M N O P Q R S T U V W X Y Z

LET'S LEARN

The Letters

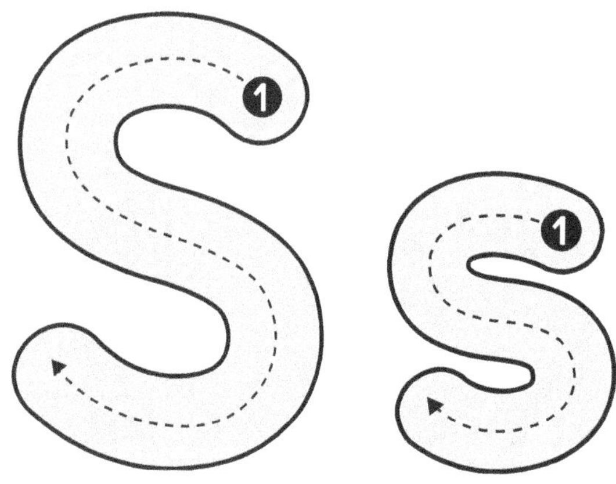

Trace the uppercase letter.

S S S S S S S S S S

S S S S S S S S S

Trace the lowercase letter.

s s s s s s s s s

s s s s s s s s s

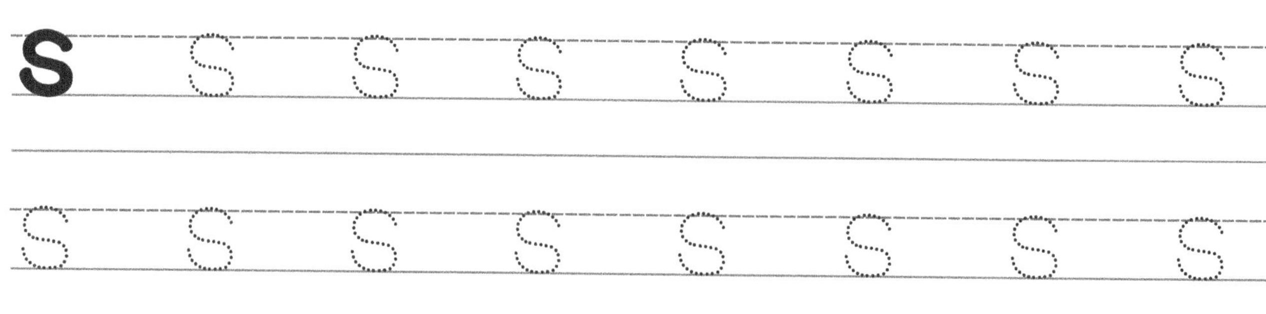

Write the uppercase letter.

S

Write the lowercase letter.

s

Trace the words that begin with letter s.

spoon spoon spoon

shoes shoes shoes

star star star

| A | B | C | D | E | F | G | H | I | J | K | L | M | N | O | P | Q | R | S | T | U | V | W | X | Y | Z |

Write the letter s on each sun.

Color the picture.

Shark

Find and color the letter S.

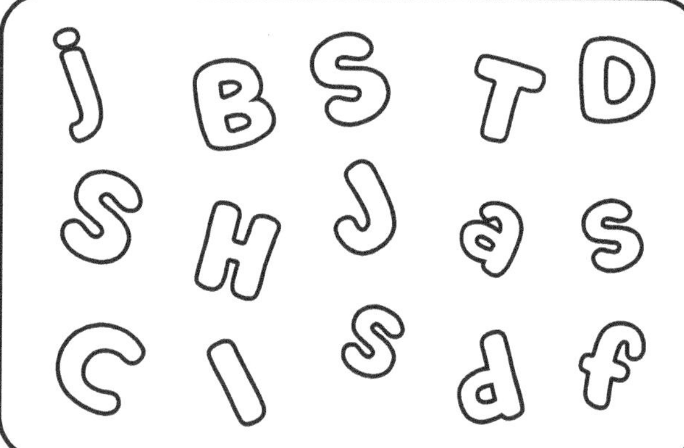

Circle the first letter for each picture.

I P S

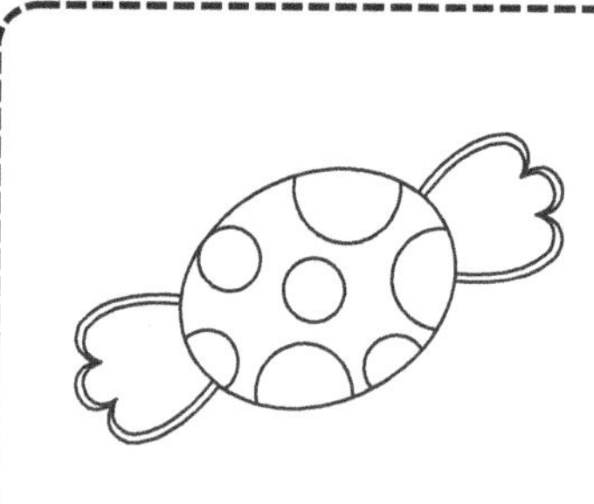

A C N

S M N

A	B	C	D	E	F	G	H	I	J	K	L	M	N	O	P	Q	R	S	T	U	V	W	X	Y	Z

LET'S LEARN
The Letters

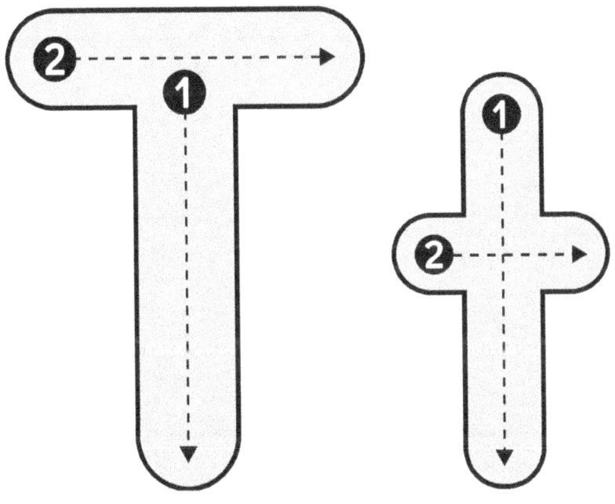

Trace the uppercase letter.

Trace the lowercase letter.

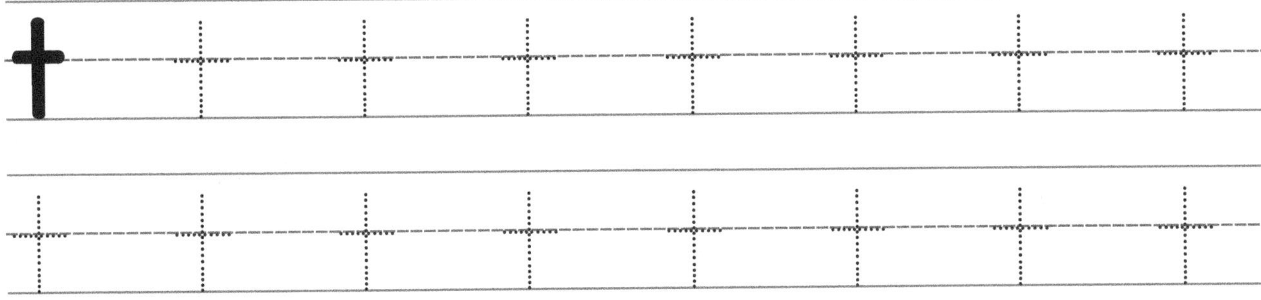

Write the uppercase letter.

T

Write the lowercase letter.

t

Trace the words that begin with letter t.

tent   tent   tent

tooth   tooth   tooth

tie   tie   tie

| A | B | C | D | E | F | G | H | I | J | K | L | M | N | O | P | Q | R | S | T | U | V | W | X | Y | Z |

Write the letter t on each turtle.

Color the picture.

Turkey

Find and color the letter T.

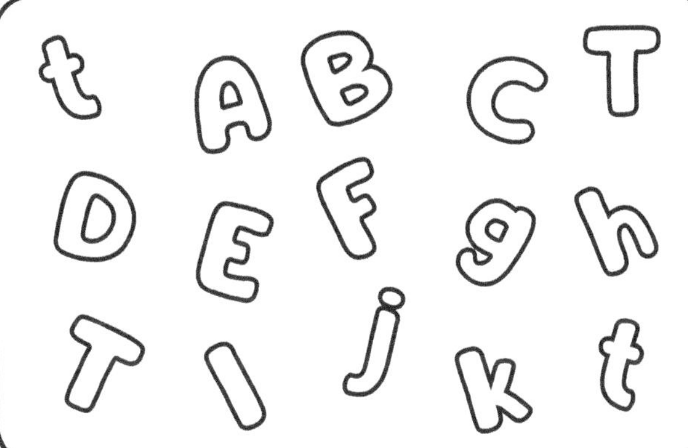

Circle the first letter for each picture.

S	T	A

N	I	T

T	E	R

A	B	C	D	E	F	G	H	I	J	K	L	M	N	O	P	Q	R	S	T	U	V	W	X	Y	Z

LET'S LEARN

The Letters

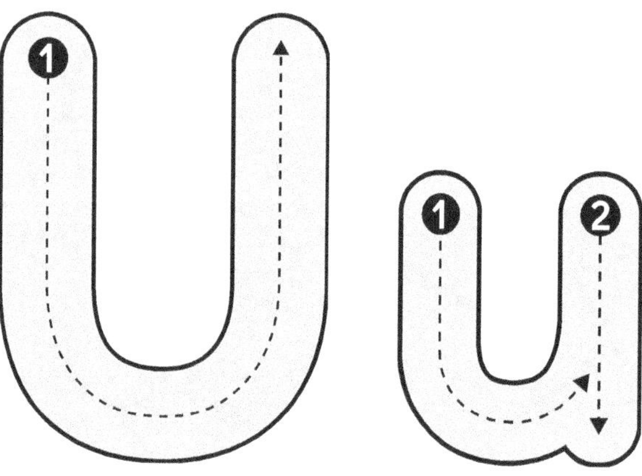

Trace the uppercase letter.

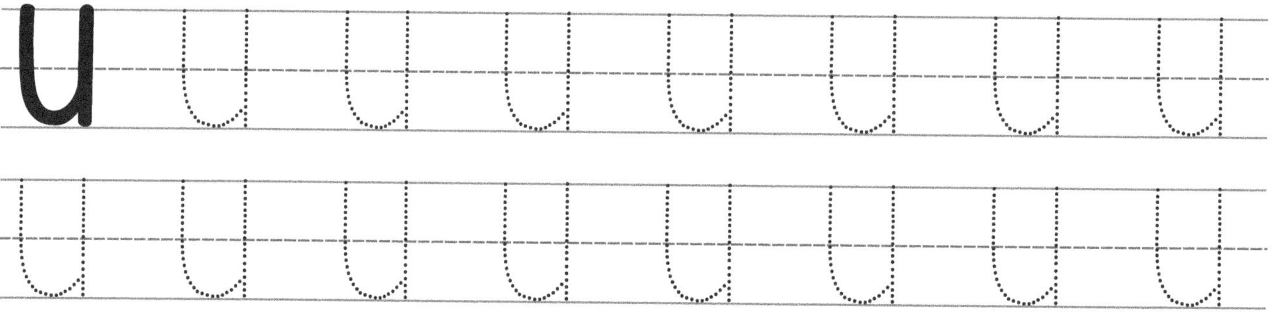

Trace the lowercase letter.

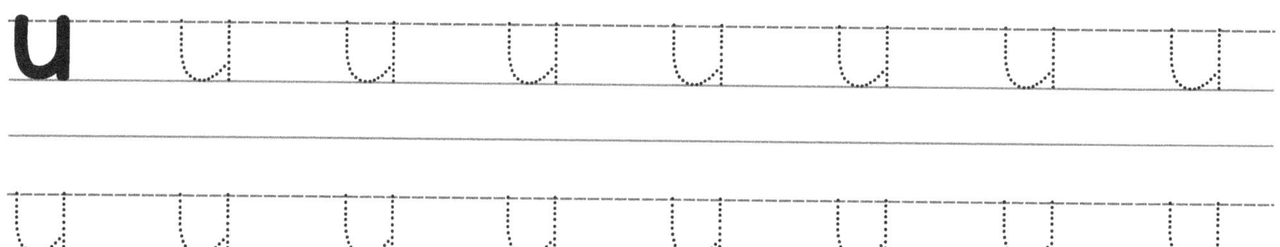

A	B	C	D	E	F	G	H	I	J	K	L	M	N	O	P	Q	R	S	T	U	V	W	X	Y	Z

Write the uppercase letter.

U

Write the lowercase letter.

u

Trace the words that begin with letter u.

uncle   uncle   uncle

ugly   ugly   ugly

urn   urn   urn

| A | B | C | D | E | F | G | H | I | J | K | L | M | N | O | P | Q | R | S | T | U | V | W | X | Y | Z |

Write the letter u on each umbrella.

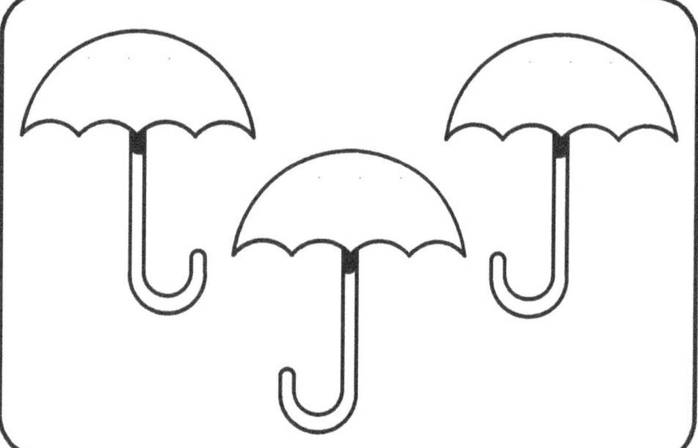

Find and color the letter U.

Color the picture.

Uniform

Circle the first letter for each picture.

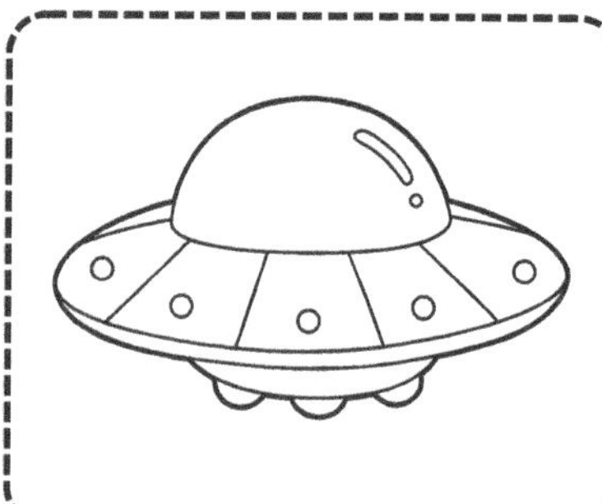

P   U   K

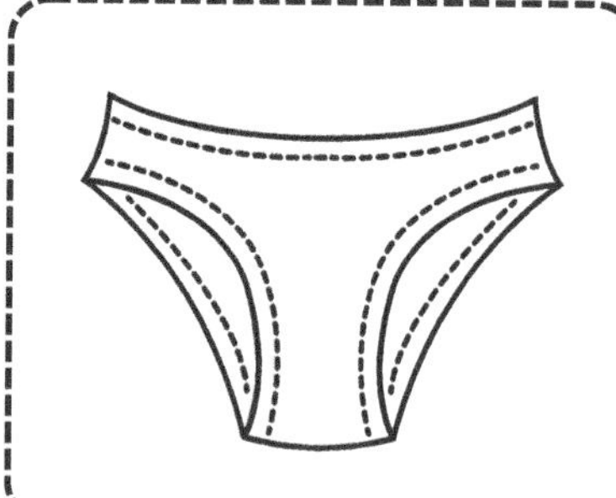

U   F   R

N   S   U

A B C D E F G H I J K L M N O P Q R S T U V W X Y Z

LET'S LEARN
THE LETTERS

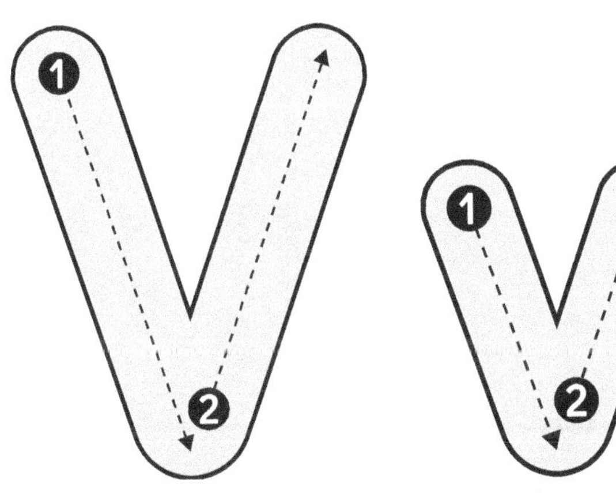

Trace the uppercase letter.

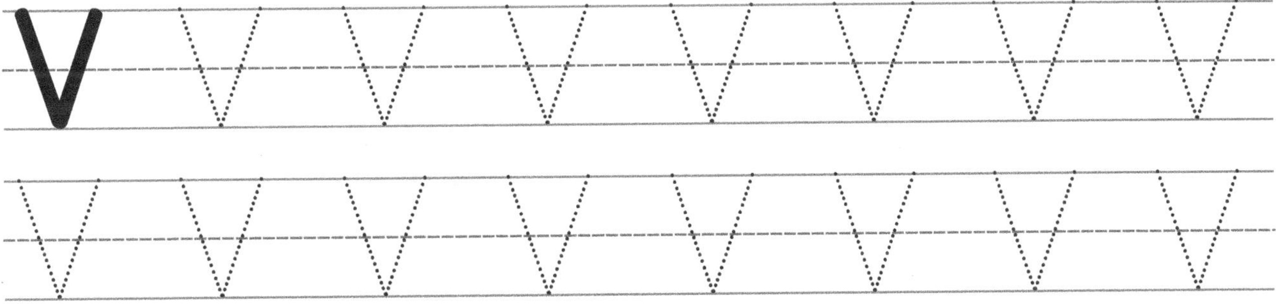

Trace the lowercase letter.

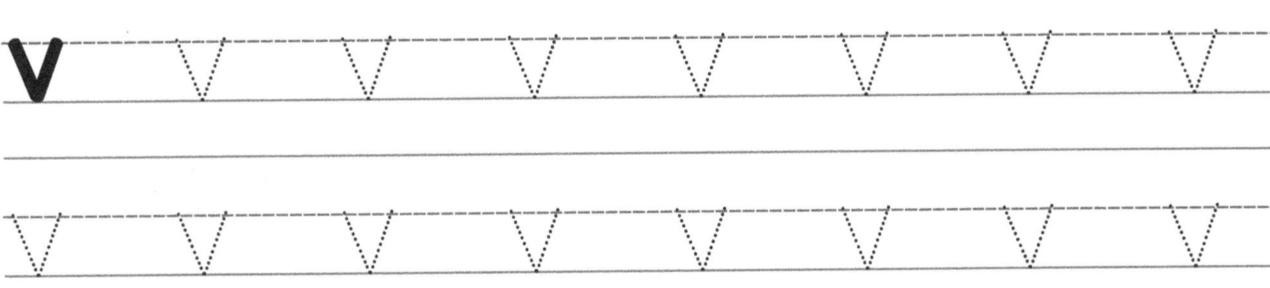

| A | B | C | D | E | F | G | H | I | J | K | L | M | N | O | P | Q | R | S | T | U | V | W | X | Y | Z |

Write the uppercase letter.

V

Write the lowercase letter.

v

Trace the words that begin with letter v.

vest   vest   vest

valley   valley   valley

violet   violet   violet

| A | B | C | D | E | F | G | H | I | J | K | L | M | N | O | P | Q | R | S | T | U | V | W | X | Y | Z |

Write the letter v on each vase.

Color the picture.

Volcano

Find and color the letter V.

Circle the first letter for each picture.

V   L   O

A   C   S

Q   P   V

| A | B | C | D | E | F | G | H | I | J | K | L | M | N | O | P | Q | R | S | T | U | V | W | X | Y | Z |

LET'S LEARN
The Letters

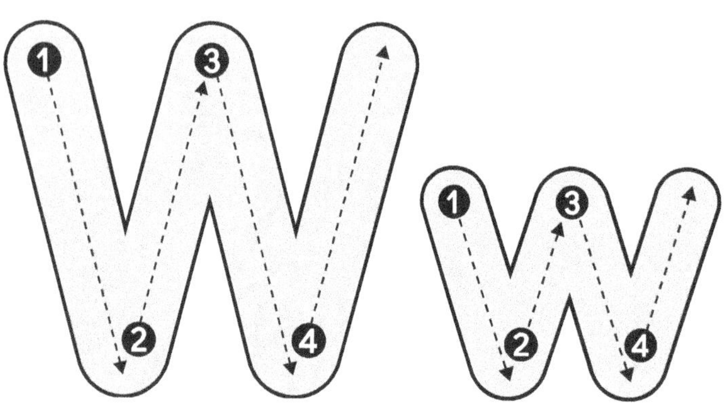

Trace the uppercase letter.

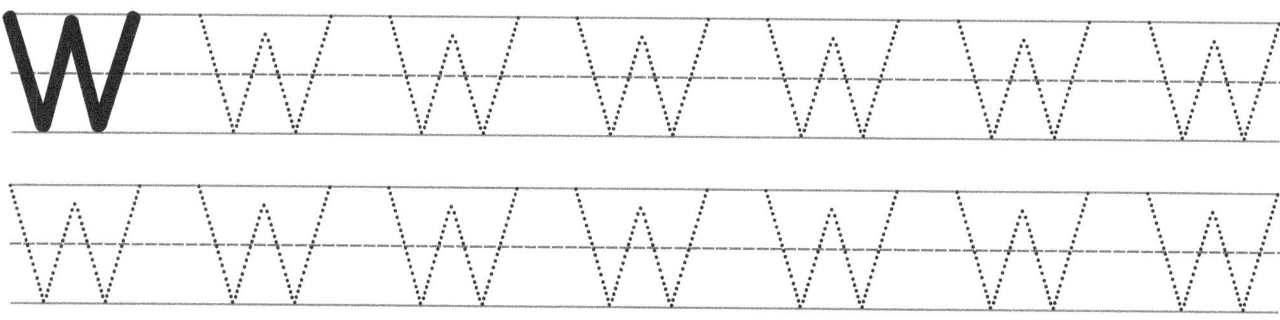

Trace the lowercase letter.

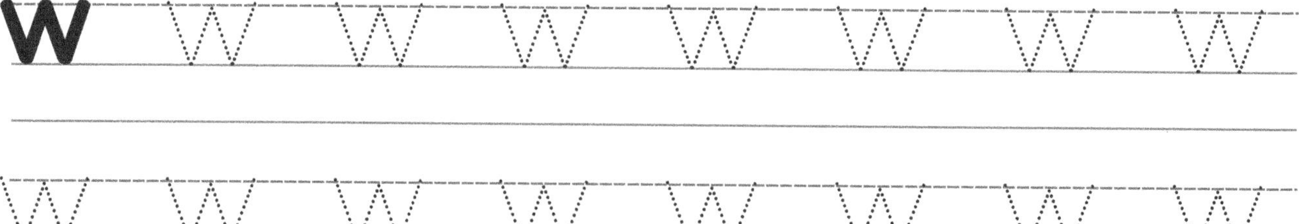

A	B	C	D	E	F	G	H	I	J	K	L	M	N	O	P	Q	R	S	T	U	V	W	X	Y	Z

Write the uppercase letter.

W

Write the lowercase letter.

w

Trace the words that begin with letter w.

wave   wave   wave

wall   wall   wall

web   web   web

| A | B | C | D | E | F | G | H | I | J | K | L | M | N | O | P | Q | R | S | T | U | V | W | X | Y | Z |

Write the letter w on each window.

Color the picture.

Find and color the letter W.

Witch

Circle the first letter for each picture.

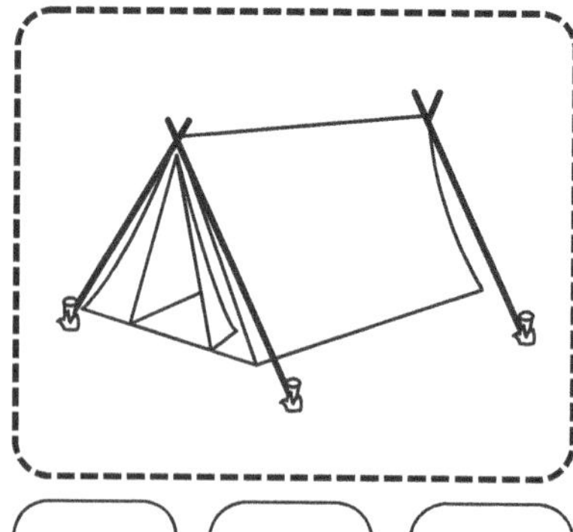

| W | T | E | | M | T | W | | L | W | F |

| A | B | C | D | E | F | G | H | I | J | K | L | M | N | O | P | Q | R | S | T | U | V | W | X | Y | Z |

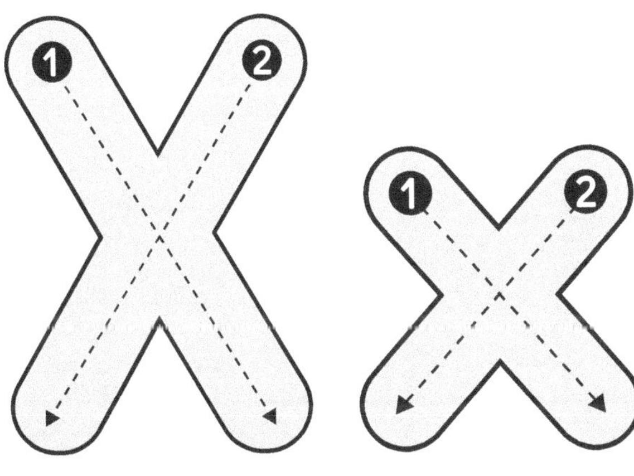

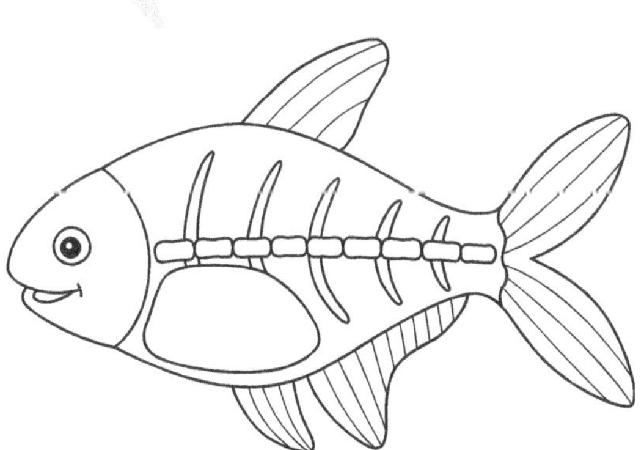

Trace the uppercase letter.

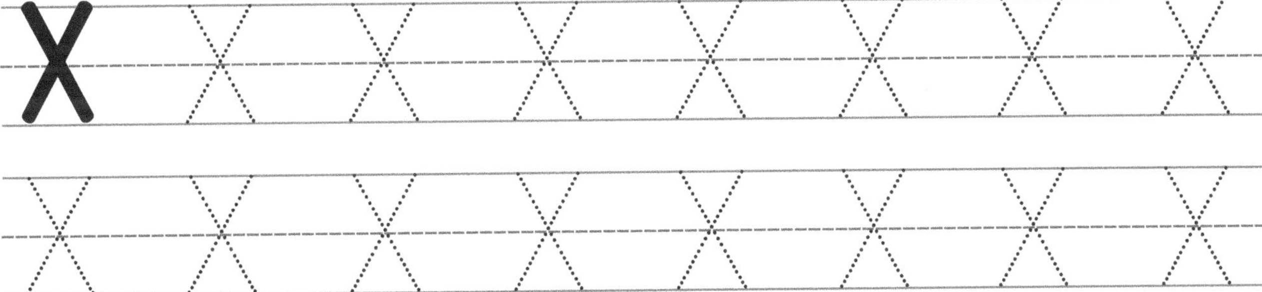

Trace the lowercase letter.

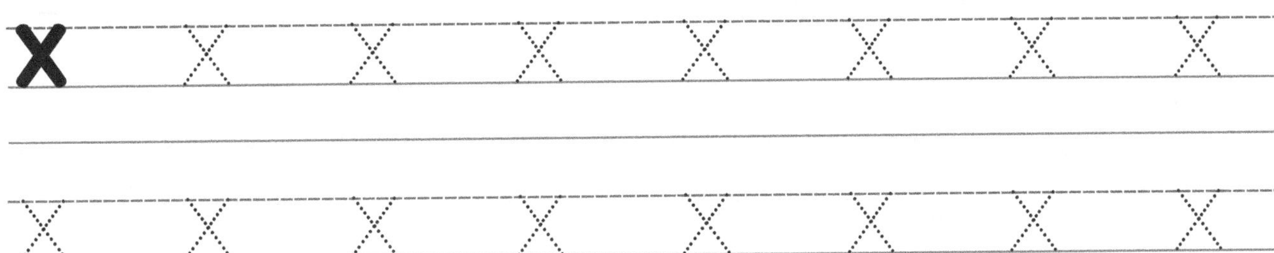

X

x

Trace the words that begin with letter x.

xmax xmax xmax

X-ray X-ray X-ray

Xerus Xerus Xerus

| A | B | C | D | E | F | G | H | I | J | K | L | M | N | O | P | Q | R | S | T | U | V | W | X | Y | Z |

Write the letter x on each ximenia.

Color the picture.

Find and color the letter X.

Circle the first letter for each picture.

A	C	B

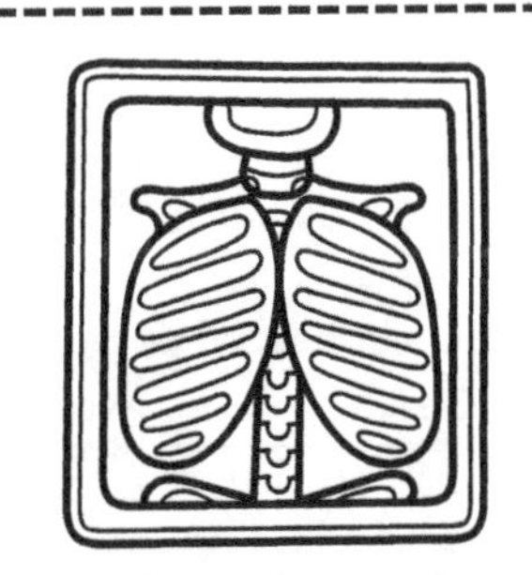

S	W	X

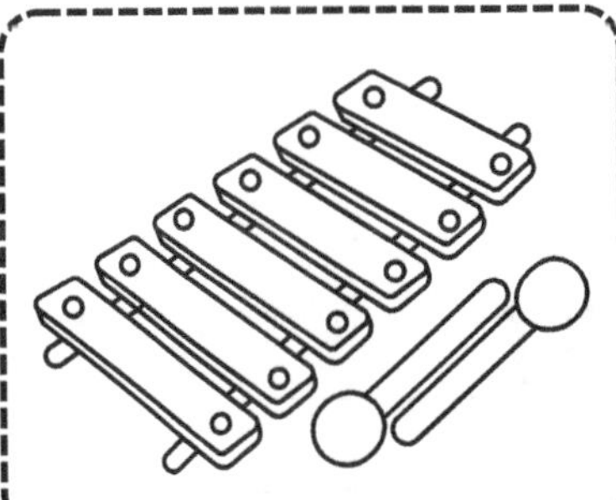

X	Q	U

A B C D E F G H I J K L M N O P Q R S T U V W X Y Z

LET'S LEARN
The Letters

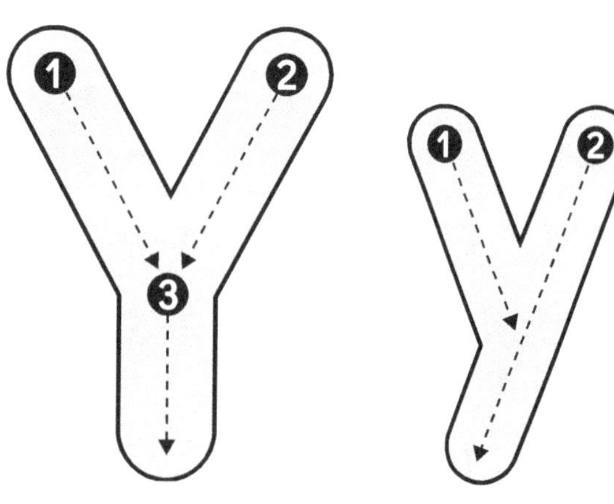

Trace the uppercase letter.

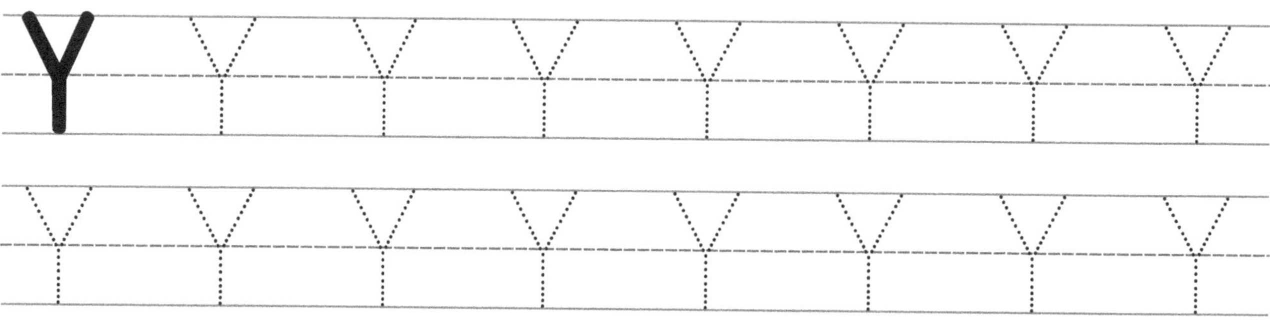

Trace the lowercase letter.

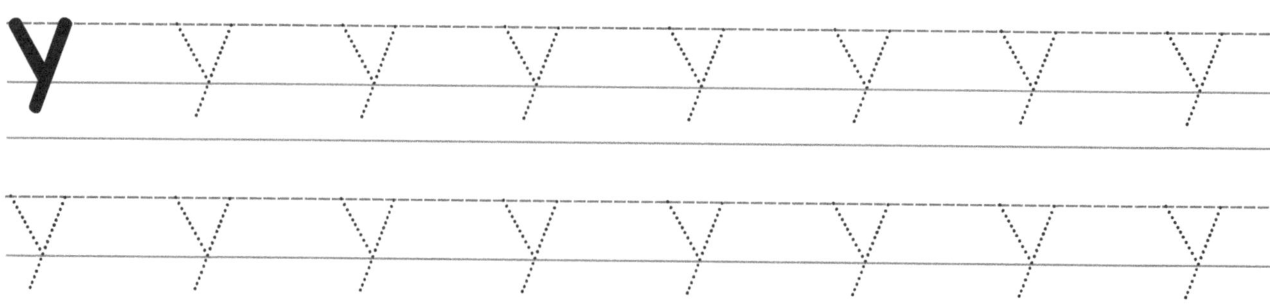

A	B	C	D	E	F	G	H	I	J	K	L	M	N	O	P	Q	R	S	T	U	V	W	X	Y	Z

Write the uppercase letter.

Y

Write the lowercase letter.

y

Trace the words that begin with letter y.

yoga   yoga   yoga

yolk   yolk   yolk

yam   yam   yam

A B C D E F G H I J K L M N O P Q R S T U V W X Y Z

Write the letter y on each yo-yo.

Color the picture.

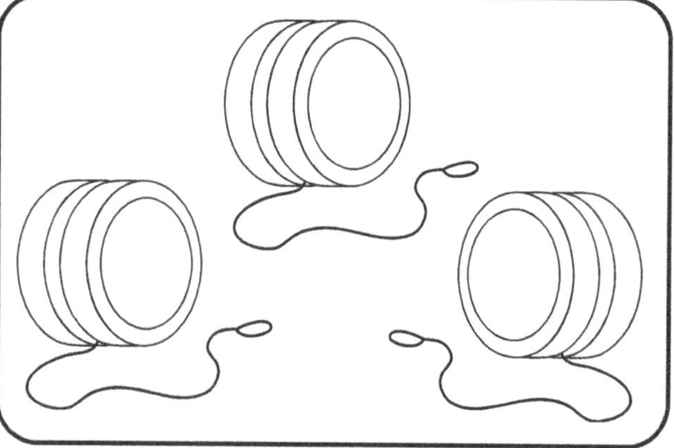

Find and color the letter Y.

Yarn

Circle the first letter for each picture.

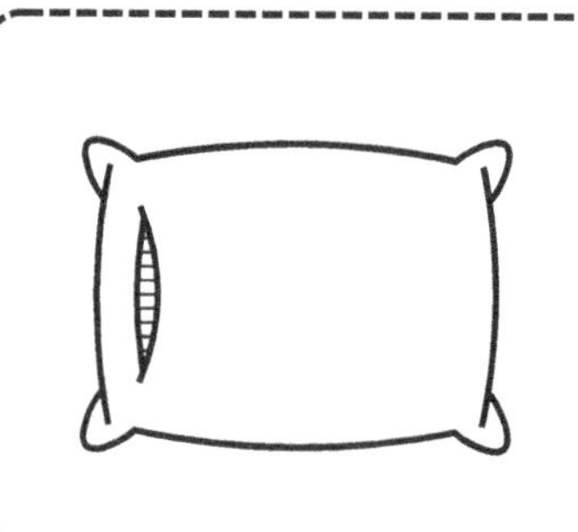

| Y | A | H |

| G | Y | T |

| O | L | P |

LET'S LEARN
The Letters

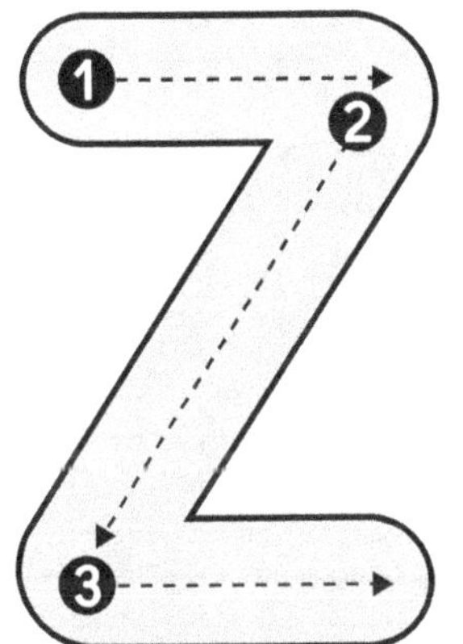

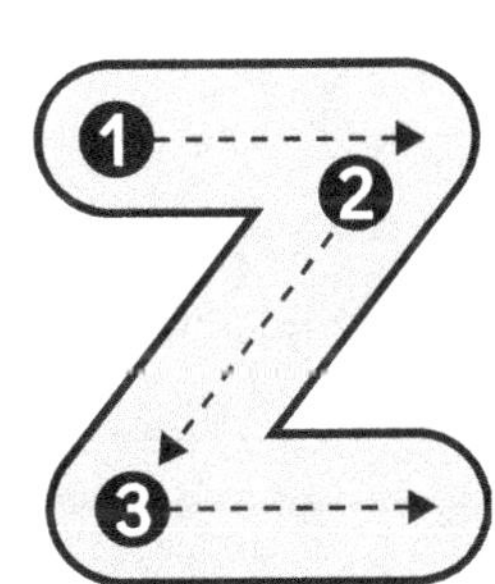

Trace the uppercase letter.

Z

Trace the lowercase letter.

z

| A | B | C | D | E | F | G | H | I | J | K | L | M | N | O | P | Q | R | S | T | U | V | W | X | Y | Z |

Write the uppercase letter.

Z

Write the lowercase letter.

z

Trace the words that begin with letter z.

zero   zero   zero

zinnia   zinnia   zinnia

zoo   zoo   zoo

| A | B | C | D | E | F | G | H | I | J | K | L | M | N | O | P | Q | R | S | T | U | V | W | X | Y | Z |

Write the letter z on each zeppelin.

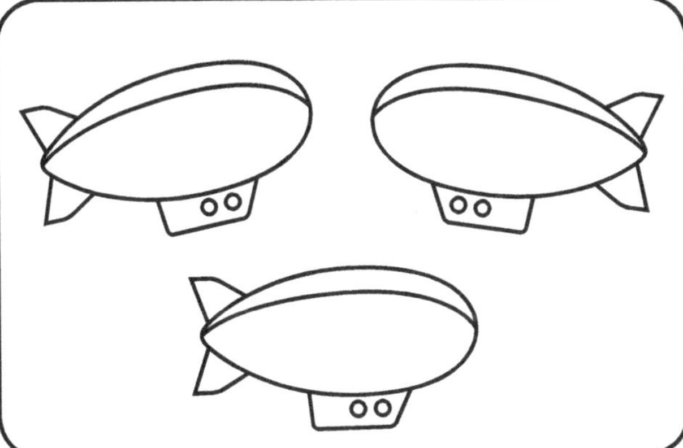

Find and color the letter Z.

Color the picture.

Zombie

Circle the first letter for each picture.

Z	I	N

J	G	Z

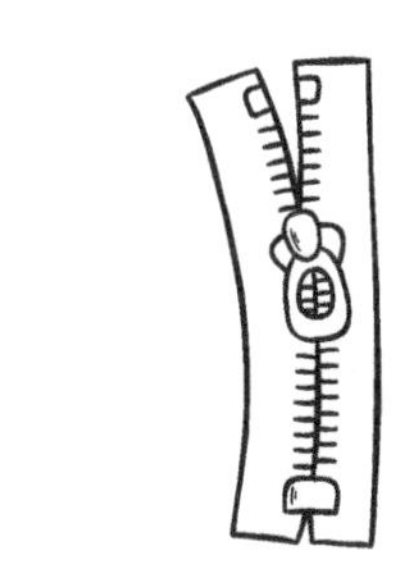

R	Z	I

A B C D E F G H I J K L M N O P Q R S T U V W X Y **Z**

LET'S LEARN
The Letters

Trace the uppercase letters.

LET'S LEARN
The Letters

Trace the lowercase letters.

LET'S LEARN

The Letters

Trace the uppercase and lowercase letters.

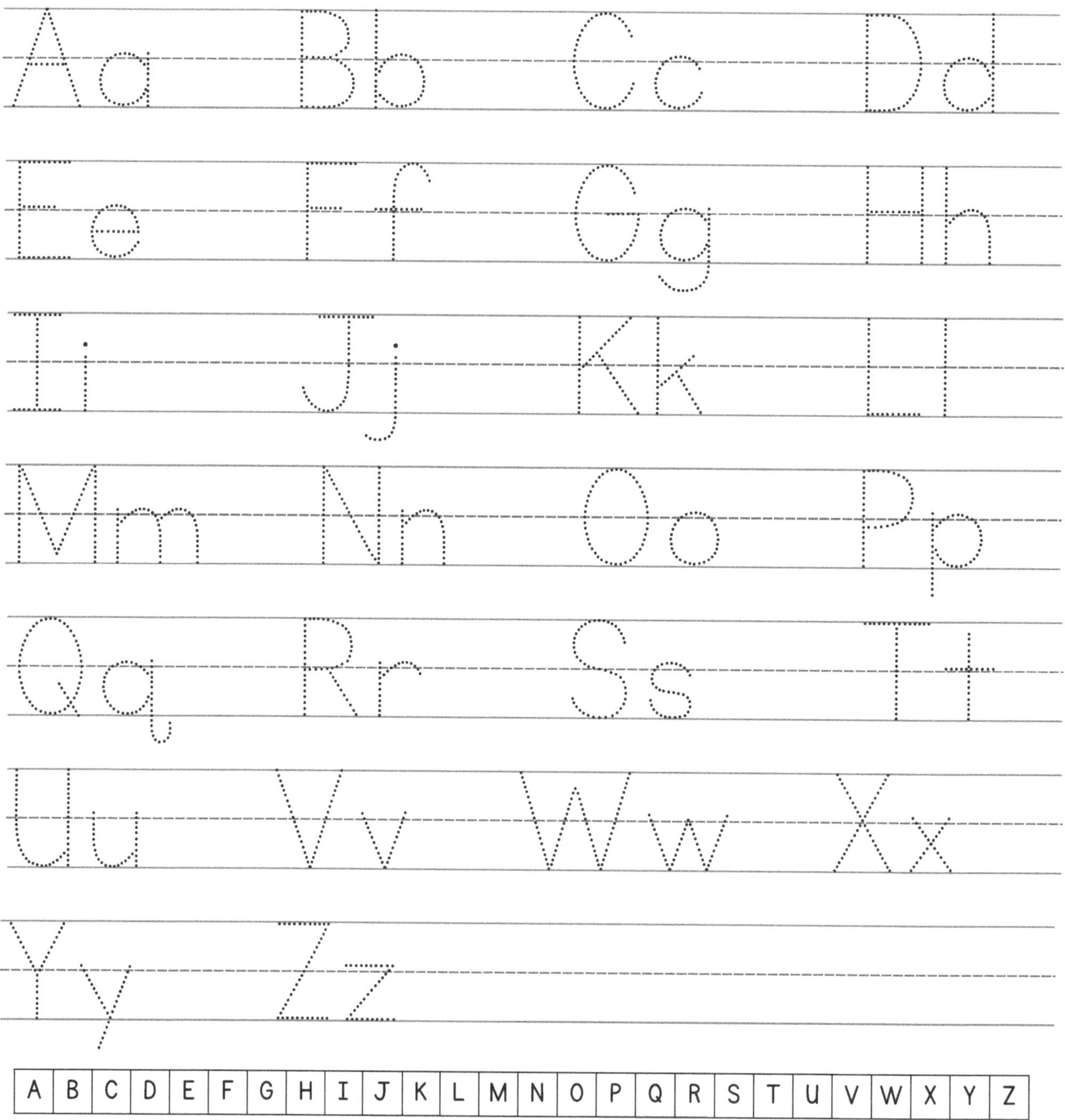

LET'S LEARN
Sentence Writing

Trace the dotted letters to practice writing the sentences.

It is a car.

It is a cat.

It is a boy.

| A | B | C | D | E | F | G | H | I | J | K | L | M | N | O | P | Q | R | S | T | U | V | W | X | Y | Z |

LET'S LEARN
Sentence Writing

Trace the dotted letters to practice writing the sentences.

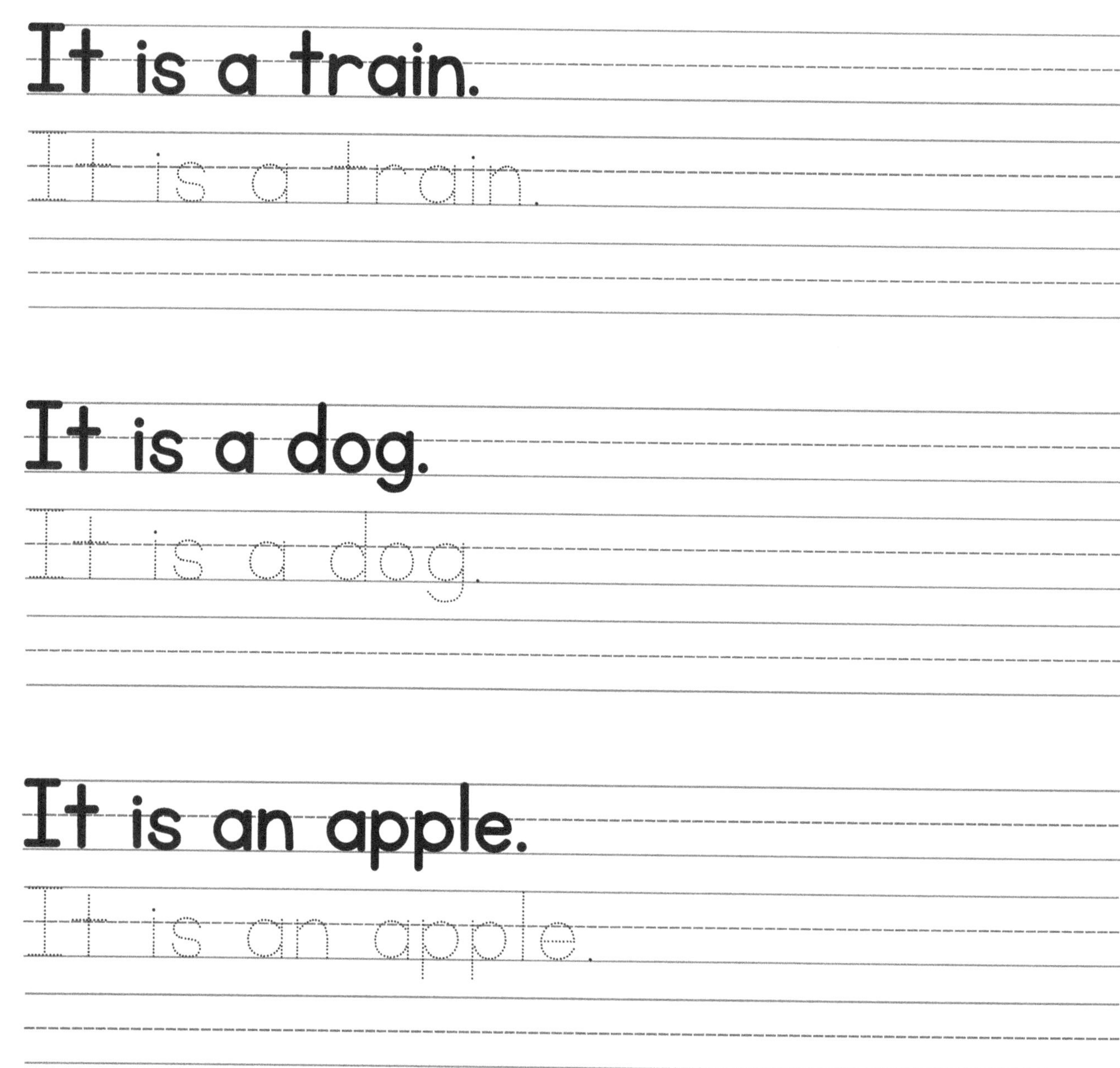

| A | B | C | D | E | F | G | H | I | J | K | L | M | N | O | P | Q | R | S | T | U | V | W | X | Y | Z |

LET'S LEARN
Sentence Writing

Trace the dotted letters to practice writing the sentences.

I like apples.

I like apples.

I like oranges.

I like oranges.

I like bananas.

I like bananas.

| A | B | C | D | E | F | G | H | I | J | K | L | M | N | O | P | Q | R | S | T | U | V | W | X | Y | Z |

LET'S LEARN
Sentence Writing

Trace the dotted letters to practice writing the sentences.

I like pineapples.

I like pineapples.

I like mangoes.

I like mangoes.

I like grapes.

I like grapes.

| A | B | C | D | E | F | G | H | I | J | K | L | M | N | O | P | Q | R | S | T | U | V | W | X | Y | Z |

LET'S LEARN
Sentence Writing

Trace the dotted letters to practice writing the sentences.

I like corn.

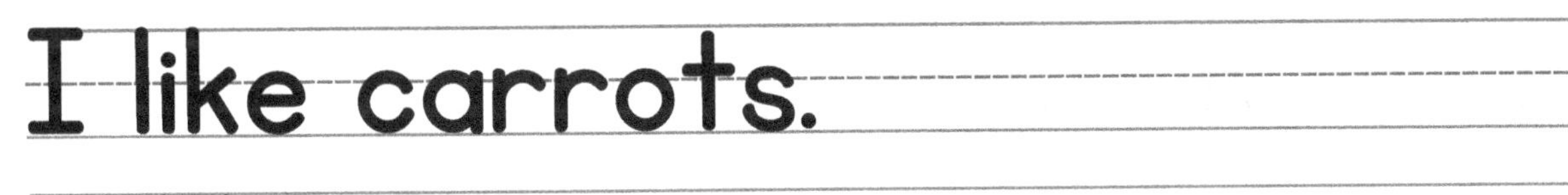

I like carrots.

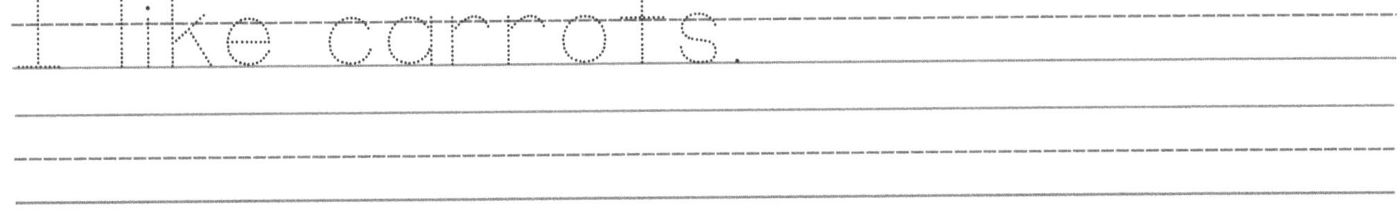

I like tomatoes.

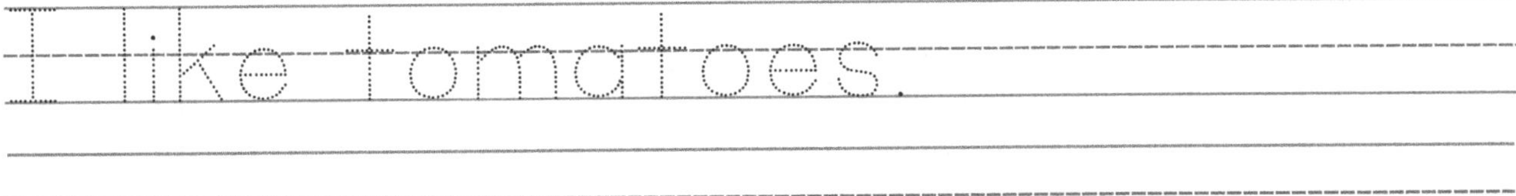

A	B	C	D	E	F	G	H	I	J	K	L	M	N	O	P	Q	R	S	T	U	V	W	X	Y	Z

LET'S LEARN

Sentence Writing

Trace the dotted letters to practice writing the sentences.

I like broccoli.

I like broccoli.

I like pumpkins.

I like pumpkins.

I like eggplants.

I like eggplants.

| A | B | C | D | E | F | G | H | I | J | K | L | M | N | O | P | Q | R | S | T | U | V | W | X | Y | Z |

LET'S LEARN

Alphabet Order

Fill in the missing letters.

A	B		D		F
G		I		K	L
M			P	Q	R
	T	U	V		X
	Z				

LET'S LEARN
Match The Letters

Draw a line to match the uppercase letter on the left to its lowercase letter on the right.

f •	• A	k •	• M
d •	• F	h •	• N
c •	• E	l •	• K
b •	• D	i •	• O
g •	• G	o •	• L
f •	• C	j •	• I
a •	• F	m •	• J
e •	• B	n •	• H

LET'S LEARN

Dot-to-dot

Sing the ABC's as you draw the fish. Color it.

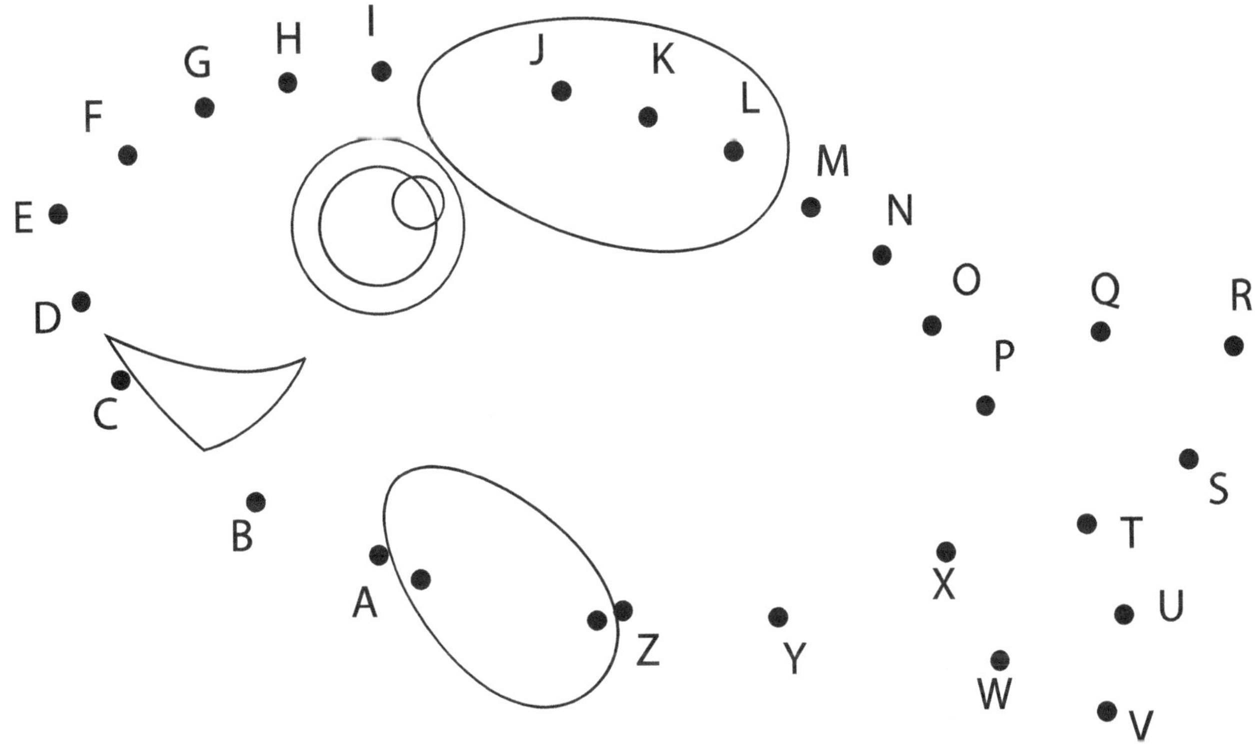

LET'S LEARN

Dot-to-dot

Sing the ABC's as you draw the whale. Color it.

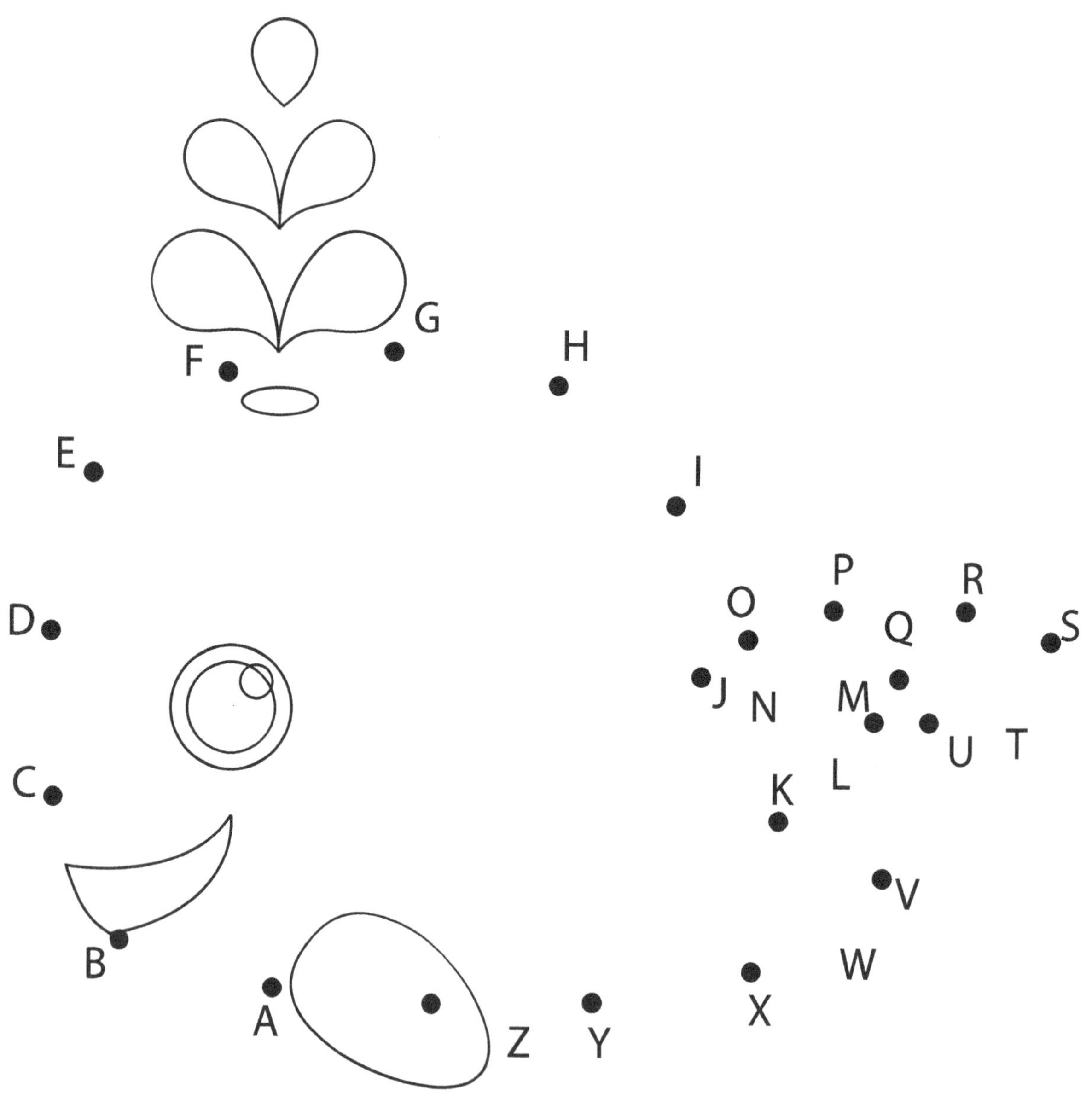

LET'S LEARN

Jumbled Words

Look at the picture, then arrange the words correctly!

LET'S LEARN

Jumbled Words

Look at the picture, then arrange the words correctly!

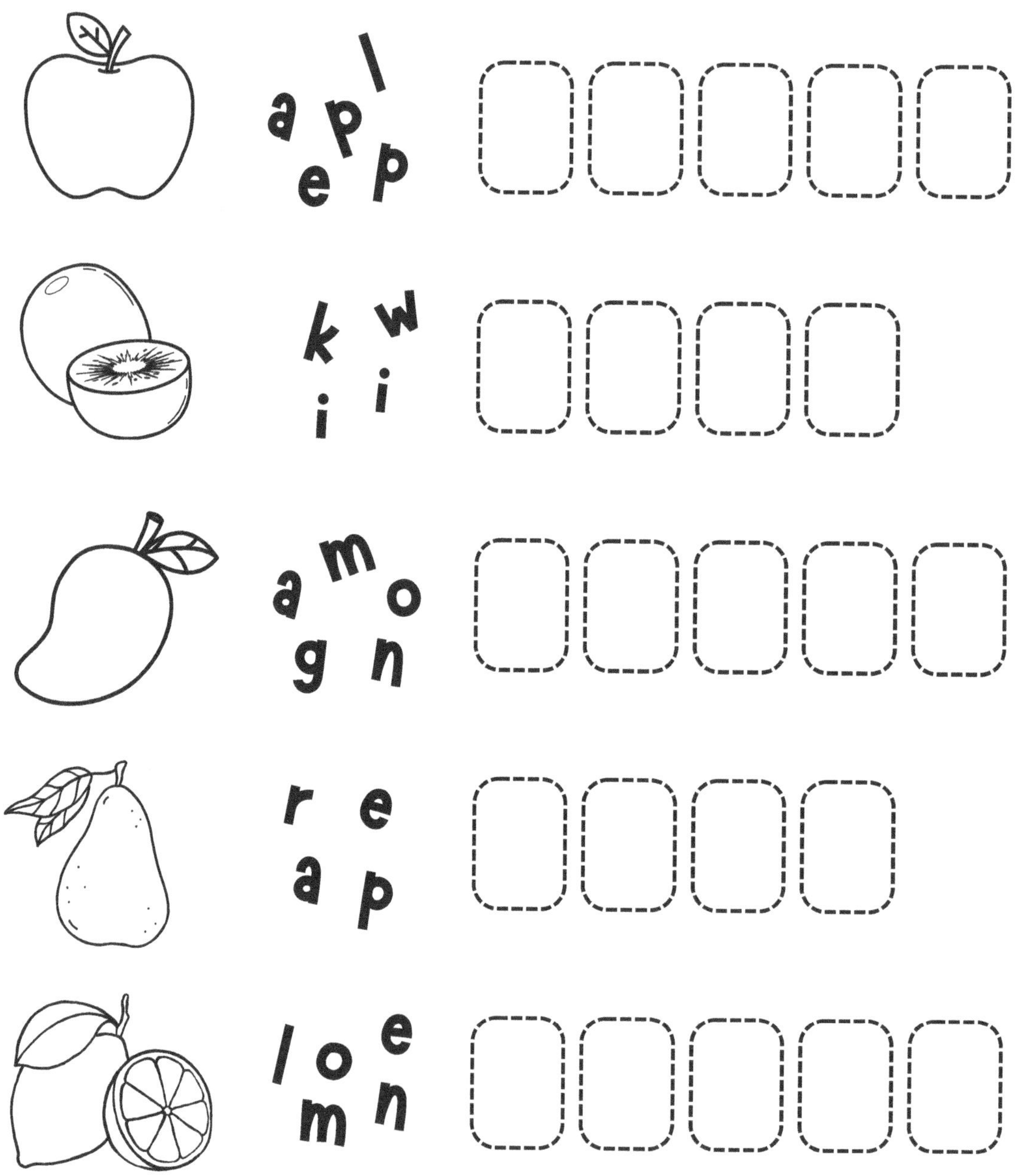

LET'S LEARN

Jumbled Words

Look at the picture, then arrange the words correctly!

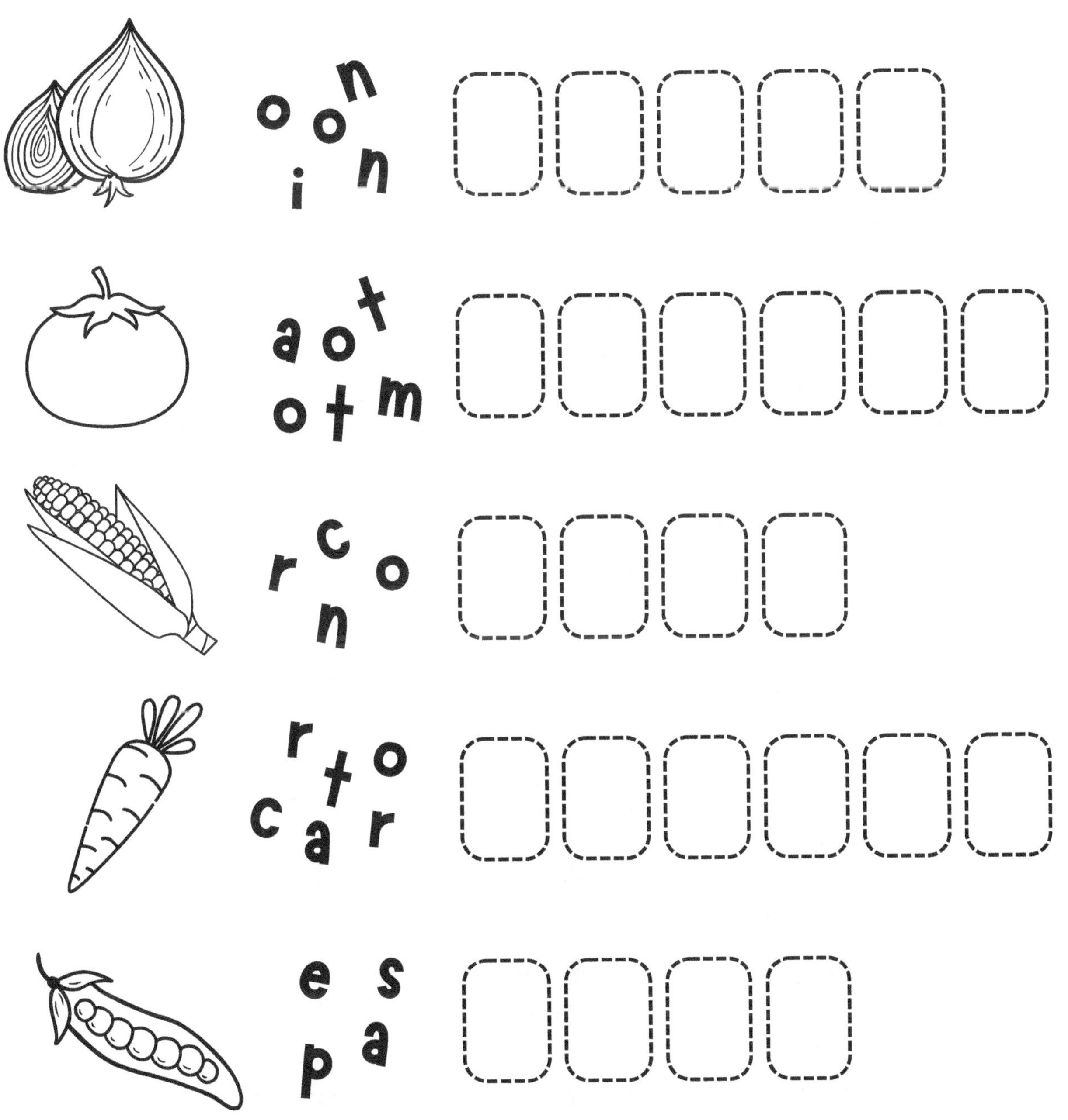

LET'S LEARN

Word Search

Find and write the 6 hidden words. Words can be found across and down.

o	d	v	a	c	s
g	f	a	s	a	d
f	a	n	q	t	t
a	b	a	g	y	n
g	w	n	m	a	p

sad

van

map

bag

fan

cat

LET'S LEARN

Word Search

Find and write the 6 hidden words. Words can be found across and down.

d	i	g	b	u	s
c	u	t	a	n	e
b	e	s	u	n	t
u	a	t	o	x	u
n	o	m	u	g	b

bus
cut
sun
tub
mug
bun

LET'S LEARN

Word Search

Find and write the 6 hidden words. Words can be found across and down.

d	b	v	p	p	i	n
i	f	l	e	g	k	
p	i	g	t	f	f	
a	l	i	d	i	i	
k	i	n	w	g	n	

dip
lid
fig
pig
pin
fin